Christian & Liz,
Thank you for all of your support! God bless you on your journey!
Rhonda Maydwell
(Mom)

a collection of inspirational stories

CONTRIBUTORS

DiAnne Malone, Editor in Chief

Hope LeNoir, Managing Editor

Demetria Bowers-Adair

Hiedi Emily

Rhonda Maydwell

Carmen Patton

Ciera Shannon

Tennessee

This publication contains the opinions and ideas of its contributing authors. It is sold with the understanding that neither the authors nor the publisher is engaged in rendering professional advice or services. If the reader requires such advice or services, a competent professional should be consulted. Relevant laws vary from state to state. The commentary outlined in this book may not be suitable for every individual, and is not guaranteed or warranted to produce any particular results.

No warranty is made with respect to the accuracy or completeness of the information contained herein, and the contributing authors along with the publisher specifically disclaim any responsibility for any liability, loss or risk, personal or otherwise, which is incurred as a consequence, directly or indirectly, of the use and application of any contents of this book.

Copyright © 2016 by DiAnne Malone

All rights reserved.
Published in the United Sates by DiAnne Malone
Printed by Create Space an Amazon.com Company
www.createspace.com

Originally published in the United States.

ISBN-13: 978-1537763514
ISBN-10: 1537763512

Printed in the United States of America

Cover design by DiAnne L. Malone
Front and back cover photography by Michael Grayson

First Paperback Edition

The story is in us, and all we have to do is sit there and write it down. But it's right about there, right about when we sit down to write that story, that things fall apart...so, by virtue of reading over what [we] have written [we] [are] forced to understand [ourselves].
ANN PATCHETT

I want very much to see you and give you some spiritual gift to make your faith stronger. I mean that I want us to help each other with the faith that we have. Your faith will help me, and my faith will help you.
THE APOSTLE PAUL
Romans 1:11, 12 ERV

CONTENTS

FORWARD: Zina S Henry, LPC	**9**
INTRODUCTION: DiAnne L. Malone	**11**
THE WORDS	
Her	13
Shoes	33
Anger	49
Image	67
Him	91
Help	109
Sexy	131
THE CUTTING ROOM FLOOR	**148**
AUTHOR BIOS	**171**
Demetria Bowers-Adair	173
Hiedi Emily	174
Hope LeNoir, Managing Editor	176
DiAnne L. Malone, Editor-in-Chief	178
Rhonda Maydwell	180
Carmen Patton	182
Ciera Shannon	184

FORWARD

By Zine S. Henry, LPC

I am elated to witness yet another publication from DiAnne and the collaboration of six other wonderful women. Surely, you will not be disappointed as you experience their different points of view on a singular word. Join these seven beautiful spirits as they reveal their souls to you in the luxury of your own home.

I first met DiAnne in 2006 at church. Right away we developed a special bond and later found out just how much we have in common. We are both English majors. We are both married. We both enjoy literature. We share a love of teaching. We can talk for hours about anything and usually do just that.

Another extension of our friendship is DiAnne's blog, "Who's That Lady," where I contribute to the marriage column. The collection of essays you hold in your hand is a spinoff from the blog and a testament to how DiAnne is gifted to bring women, their different perspectives, the art of story-telling and ministry all under one roof.

Never one to shy away from a challenge, DiAnne was determined to transfer the inspiration that many of the writers within this collection have brought to her blog to the pages of a book. I was intrigued with the project, and while I found myself unable to commit the time needed for it, I was certainly excited about it. I know it will be a blessing to any woman fortunate enough to hold a copy in her hand.

INTRODUCTION

By DiAnne L. Malone, Managing Editor

Summer 2016. Seven women boarded one plane and two SUV's to see each other, truly see each other. They knew not what to expect, even though each held an expectation. There were essays carefully packed away in their bags, folders, and attachés, precious cargo for the journey.

They had been given words, the very tools by which the world was spoken into existence. Into these words, life was to be breathed. Each woman's experience gave every word a different kind of life, life that encourages others from diverse backgrounds, communities, experiences, and occupations.

When they met, it was evident they were not afraid of each other or the baggage the words carried. They were not afraid of the hot tears that would slip through their lower lashes, melt their mascara and decorate their cheeks with flecks and shadowy streaks of black.

When they read their offerings, some of the sentences stuck at the cliffs of their throats, choked back by pain they thought they'd managed and wounds they thought were healed. The memories of one woman snatched open the door to another woman's heart, found a cluttered chamber, and took a seat.

The seven women hunkered down in the living room where they met to commune. Some sat on the shiny hard wood floors; others were wrapped in colorful knitted quilts which, at first sight, they'd claimed as their own. One held the life of another in her belly, but still struggled sacrificially through the pruning process of editing. One tried not to cry and did. Others cried and could not stop. The couches cradled each woman's story as a mother carrying her first baby.

From the sharing of words and the life within, a sisterhood took hold among the seven souls. It shook them with excitement and anticipation. Worship of a different ilk was experienced. They worshiped through story.

The stories are sweet and tender, hard to hear, difficult to manage, embarrassing, hilarious, and sometimes too private to share, like secrets between best friends — not the kind of stories you hear in Bible study.

These stories contain cussing uncles, violated children, the single jar of Miracle Whip an abusive husband left behind, the day when the N-word changed a child's life, the child who was kept, and the one who's vision changed forever, hearts torn into and not repaired, not yet.

Bible studies summarize. There are minimal plot points and insufficient smatterings of descriptive scenes translated as a message with just enough ambiguity to keep one wondering what really happened. These women say what really happened, without flinching, without looking away. Each story is a true story--riveting in simplicity, vulnerable in delivery, heartbreaking, uplifting and heavy with truth. They build a ladder to the shelves of emotions that seem too high to reach.

These seven women, stand on their tippy toes, pull out their pens and write each word, as they dangle dangerously from the rungs, with love to each woman reading.

Her

"She conjures up ghosts from the fringes of her mind, gives them skin, and calls me by their names."

−DiAnne Malone

Hiedi Emily

Women tend to rush to put others first. We nurture children, lose sleep for friends, and lay down our dreams to invest in the dreams of our men. We praise and serve God, and can get our "warrior princess "on if we sense injustice or think our family is being attacked. We stay late at work to get the job done and please our employers. We stay up late and get up early to squeeze more into every day. Often we arrive at a place of frustrated exhaustion wondering how we ended up strapped onto this crazy merry-go-round, and if there's a way to get off. We leave no room for her. The her who can take control and stop this crazy thing.

Her, simply defined, is a three letter feminine possessive pronoun. A seemingly insignificant, filler word in countless reports, articles, and books. But it's so much more. Because it's possessive in nature it shows connection and election. It's a choice, a declaration, an example, a hope.

Her family; her style; her convictions; her perspective; her friends; her laughter; her tears; her education; her feelings; her dreams - they all stem from the heart and soul of a woman.

Her frenzy also tends to leave her in a place where she uses her possessive pronoun incorrectly. Her insecurities, her failures, her worries, her wrinkles and cellulite, her fears, her self-criticism and self-loathing. How many women do you know that are filled with self-doubt? Women who feel like they're not successful enough, pretty enough, talented enough, or good enough mothers, wives, or daughters?

In the hectic pace of twenty-first century life we often feel like we have no choices, as if they've been stripped away from us. It's like life just happened, and to keep all the proverbial balls up in the air we need to just keep moving — that there is no room for the idealism we vaguely remember having when we were younger.

What if each woman made her choice — one that reclaims that very option? What if choosing to value herself and her thoughts and dreams was the path to freedom?

Her life will be more fulfilled, happier, and a greater blessing to all the loved ones for whom she has routinely sacrificed for when she chooses to see her destiny as a well-balanced collage of her faith, her family, her man's goals, her friend's interests, her career's success, community's needs, *and* her personal passions.

By choosing to prioritize her dreams, every woman gives more than she ever could by denying them. This is true because alongside her devotion and duty she gives her shining example and her testimony. The Word says, we overcome "by the blood of the Lamb, and by the word of [our] testimony" (Rev. 12:11). When God empowers one to achieve, He sets the precedent that He's willing to do it for all.

Psalm 37:4 says, "delight yourself in the Lord and he will give you the desires of your heart." A few years ago God gave me the revelation that this doesn't mean we have a magic formula that if I am close enough to Him, He'll grant my wishes like the Lord's some kind of happy genie. When I'm submitted to Him, He actually places His desires in my heart. When they come alive inside me, and I make them my own, He can and will answer those prayers with a yes and amen because I want His will!

What if her destiny pursued inspires others to take a chance? What if in the ups and downs of choosing to chase her dreams, she teaches her children to take risks to achieve?

Let's put a generic woman aside and get really personal. What if *you* took possession of *your* dreams again? What if *I* did? How would that change your world and mine? More importantly, how would it change yours and my self-esteem, and satisfaction in life?

God gave us freewill to choose. Choose to proudly possess your hopes and dreams! Take time for you, your development, and to take at least one small step every week to own and pursue your dreams. Healthy, confident women inspire the same in others. Her dreams, her vision, her passion realized makes a way for her shining example to become her legacy.

Inspirational Writings
DiAnne Malone

I shouldn't compare myself to other women. But these women, the women in my family, are the scaffolding for womanhood to which every woman should aspire.

Each day, I watch a strong tower of that femininity fall away, stone by sturdy stone, they loosen from a once cemented life. That is not the bad part. The bad part is, I feel my feet will never grow big enough to fit the shoes they leave behind. I'm mad. Not, sad about it.

They don't even know it. For some, it is too late for me to tell them. I whisper it in my prayers or over their graves.

What they didn't mean to do was put so much pressure on me to be like them. They didn't ask that of me. They pushed me to be the best me I could be, but not a me that would make me like them.

They, my aunts and older cousins, my grandmother, my mother, are all giants, and even from the other side of this world, their fierce way of living continues to sing out to me, and now I have my own daughter to whom I hope I can pass on a kernel of their greatness.

It overwhelms me. My efforts are forced sometimes. Scripted and contrived. I want to fully be all of the women that have made me the woman I am. I want to know I'm doing right by them. I need confirmation. A whisper in my spirit. A settling in my bones. Am I close to being those women to the girl I'm raising to be a woman?

"I know who you want to be like when you grow up," my oldest son says to my youngest and only daughter (because he knows things—he knows everything).

"Who?" she asks while wiggling a loose tooth in the front of her mouth.

"You want to be just like momma." He glares at her, as if his intimidating posture will make her give the right answer. The one he thought I wanted to hear. "You want to be like, momma, right?"

"Nope," she says frankly, not at all moved by his hovering.

"You don't wanna be like momma?" He pried.

My heart was dropping, fast.

"No!" she exclaimed. "I told you; I don't want to be like momma." And back to the wiggly tooth she went.

"Oh. Oh. I got it... You want to be like dad, right?"

"Nope."

"You don't want to be like daddy?"

Tiny frown, "No."

"Oh, I know who you want to be like. You want to be like T.T. Hope." My son thought he had it then. He chuckled.

"Mm-mm," she shook her head.

"Well, who do you want to be like, then?"

"I want to be like myself. I want to be like, Layla. I like myself."

I put in a lot of hard work over the past five years. Now, I was the person my only daughter didn't want to be like. She had no inclination, as did I, to put her feet in another woman's shoes, my shoes, unless, of course, she's playing dress up.

But wait. I should be celebrating. At least that's what a friend told me. I didn't get it. Celebrate what? That I'm not worthy of mimicking? It's disheartening. I had lied to myself when I said I wanted a free-standing daughter, one who believed she could do and be anything she wanted, and I had lamented the sentiment I'd planted in her all along. I said what people should say about their children. I said it, but didn't want it for her. What did I want for her?

I back track. By seven, the nurturing from my biological mother was terminated by colon cancer. Not ten years later, my next mom figure, my grandmother, died. Today, my third and longest term mother may pick up the phone, hear my voice, and mistake me for my mother who died over 37 years ago. Her memory lapses and stretches and pulls at things that are no longer around. She conjures up ghosts from the fringes of her mind, gives them skin, and calls me by their names. What had I to teach from these fragmented experiences? How did my daughter get to her wonderful revelation? Why am I sad about it?

Maybe I'm not sad. Maybe I'm happy that she is self-aware, present, and emphatic about what she is becoming. Maybe I know that this awareness is the same one that will allow her to one day not reach out to hold my hand while she's taking her afternoon nap. Maybe, as I celebrate her independence, I mourn our separation. Who knows? I may just be missing her here, in this house, with me, before she's even gone.

7 Women 7 Words

Inspirational Writings
Demetria Adair

She had choices. First, she could have aborted me. During our midnight walks from Binghampton to North Memphis, fleeing from difficult living arrangements, she could have left me in a dark alley. She could have chosen to be absent, but she kept me. Fifty-four years ago is when I first met her. Of course, I don't recall the very moment I laid eyes on her, and I'm not sure if it was a joyous one; one thing is clear, from the past to the present she has always been there for me.

I must admit, growing up, I was indeed a blessed child. I always felt an abundance of love and was materially comfortable. I was always made to feel extra special, extra wanted by my grandparents and her. Now that I'm an adult I know they were over compensating to make sure I felt I had a place.

Her story with me began through what she thought was a fairytale love story; she the high school beauty and homecoming queen and he an athletic superstar, both from a family oriented community. It appeared to be the ideal relationship and out of their love for each other came me. Soon the ideal relationship turned into a horror story of physical abuse; beaten beyond recognition, fleeing danger during the night, all with me right by her side. The painful, agonizing decision was inevitable. To leave me in hands other than her own was a hard one. Now I know. I didn't then. Even though her life with him was life threatening, she had built a love for his family, especially his grandmother. It was the perfect solution, and that's where I would grow. I vividly remember her always being around even though she would have to leave and return another day. She was always there with the promise to one day take me with her and no longer have to say our Sunday goodbyes. It was hard (not because I wasn't loved by my grandparents), but because I so longed to be with her all the time.

Finally, in 1974 I was able to live with her without having to say, "see you later" on Sunday evenings. By this time, she was stable with a husband (my stepdad) and a new edition (my baby brother). As I entered junior high school I began to have these certain feelings about her; jealousy, insecurities, feelings of isolation and feelings of being out of place. How could this be? I mean I was there with her where I had dreamed for years to be. Things were cloudy, there were other people in my space with her, and she couldn't devote all her time to me like she did when she came to my grandparents' house. How dare she clutter up our world by sharing herself with others?

We made it through my high school graduation together and then I migrated back to my grandparents' house. Life was sometimes turbulent, but the one thing for sure was that she made it her business to ensure I knew she loved me. Fast forward past the immaturity and insecurities of a child from a broken mother, I can now see clearly her undying and unconditional love for me.

My mother could have allowed her less than ideal circumstances of being a single unwed mother who endured an abusive man to cause her to take the easy way out. Her choice was one that is still evident today — she kept me. She endured for me, she encouraged me, and she prayed for me. She loved me because I am her gift from God.

Inspirational Writings
Rhonda Meydwell

I do not really like her. I would call her a liar, but that isn't quite right. She is not malicious; I think she actually tries to protect me. She doesn't want others to think less of me, to question my walk with God, or to know how badly I sometimes hurt. She is happy when I am firing on all cylinders. She likes it when I impress others with my wifely or motherly nature. Nothing increases her contentedness more than when I sound really intelligent—or churchy. She likes it when I have answers for others. She pats me on the back when I make others laugh. She high-fives me when I get kudos at work. She really does root for me. She looks like me, and she sounds like me, but she isn't really me. She is Fake Me.

I will never forget the time I was on the phone with my sister, Lori. We were both fairly new Christians. She was describing difficulties that were going on in multiple areas of her life when she blurted, "I must not be as good of a Christian as you, nothing seems to work out right for me." I remember feeling gut-punched. The truth was that my first marriage was failing, having recently moved back to Missouri, I could not make friends at our new church, and I was terribly lonely. I had occasional fleeting thoughts about whether or not carbon monoxide poisoning would be as peaceful as I imagined. In short, I was in despair, and my life was in shambles. I felt immediate shame, however, because I knew exactly why my sister thought I lived an enchanted life. I never let anyone see the truth.

Shortly after the breakup of my marriage, I spoke with my pastor who told me kindly, but bluntly, "You presented an image that you had a perfect marriage, kids, and family." I had never purposefully set out to put on an act. In fact, I thought I had left plenty of clues that things were amiss in my marriage. I was shocked at everyone else being shocked.

Part of the deception was done in good-faith privacy. Even today, I do not believe spouses should slander each other or air every argument they have. Another reason for the façade was well-meaning advice from a friend who told me that sometimes we (women) just have to "fake it until we make it." In other words, if I pretended things were one way, maybe one day they actually would be. So I tried that.

All through that difficult time, I really hoped and prayed that my marriage would be healed. I bought and read a book by Lee and Leslie Strobel entitled *Surviving a Spiritual Mismatch in Marriage* in the hope of incorporating strategies to help my floundering marriage where religion was a key trouble. Excellent book, but terrible title — not too helpful when your spouse is offended by the book he finds in the bathroom… "Are you *surviving* your spiritual mismatch today, Rhonda?"

The other side of the coin, however, was my enormous pride. I liked being the good wife, the awesome mom, and the uber-godly Christian. I would rather be admired than pitied, so I put on my best face, and tried to keep all of the plates spinning for as long as I could. Some readers may remember a Billy Crystal Saturday Night Live character named Fernando. Fernando's mantra was that it is better to look good than to feel good. His over-the-top character often said, "Dahling, you look MAHVELOUS!" This was usually said to someone in an impossibly terrible situation, but Fernando always offered his sage advice to concentrate how one looks instead of how one feels. I think I was a (slightly) understated Fernando.

I was crushed by my sister's statement, however, and I felt like the world's biggest fraud. I dove into my Bible and began praying for humility and the courage to be authentic. Paul in the Bible had no trouble with authenticity when he proclaimed, "when I came to you, brothers, I did not come proclaiming to you the testimony of God with lofty speech or wisdom…I was with you in weakness and in fear and much trembling, and my speech and my message were not in plausible words of wisdom" (1Cor 2:1-5). It is still difficult for me to picture the authoritative Paul stumbling over his words as he began to build churches! The truth is, that our message is more effective in our weakness. How does it help anyone to present an unattainable image to someone trying to figure this righteousness thing out? Why wouldn't someone throw in the towel in the face of a Christian image they can't seem to attain? The Bible says, "Sanctify them in the truth" (John 17:17). As Christians, I think that if we lose the identity that "I am a lowly sinner just trying to make my way through this world, and the only thing I have going for me is that I turned my life over to Jesus," then we risk losing those whom we hope to meet in Heaven.

I work very hard to be authentic and transparent with everyone. I want to be known as a truth-teller. I still sometimes contend with *her*. She tries to intervene and offer some plastic protection from time to time. It isn't easy to be authentic, but I would rather look like a loser than to ever cause a brother or sister to stumble while trying to obtain a fake image.

7 Women 7 Words

Inspirational Writings
Ciera Shannon

She always gave me fruit and a sandwich on our walks back home. She held my hand whenever I requested. Her hugs were warm and snug. She was indeed my walking angel, standing tall in a room filled with average individuals, five-nine to be exact.

Her skin like the rich creamer you add to your coffee. Her hair, black as coal, but shiny like a rare diamond, a mole placed perfectly on the right side of her face. Her mere presence was a representation of elegance, and I could never get enough of her. Our time together was usually short but filled with fun packed activities: drawing, coloring, word puzzles. I looked forward to our lively conversations. They were filled with talks of self-confidence and reassurance. She told me I was loved.

Reminders of my unique beauty often lead our conversations. "Ciera, you know, no one has a smile like yours." She told me. So, I always smiled in her presence.

It's why I'm always smiling today. I loved her. Whenever I knew she was visiting I would make sure to wash my hands and clean my nails. She instructed, "Ladies should always have clean hands and nails."

I looked for her mole in my face, and surprisingly, I found it. It is beautifully placed slightly below my nose and above my lips. Mine is much smaller, of course, but the sight of it, made me her mini-me.

She taught me how to snap my fingers. I didn't completely grasp it at the time, but the consistent practice afterwards made it a sure victory. Imagine my surprise when I realized that I would never see her again. It was abrupt. Just like the snap of my fingers. In that swift moment when skin connects to skin and leaves a resonating sound, she became an echo.

I cried behind a chair after her funeral because I wasn't sure if I was allowed to grieve her absence. I looked at her body and wondered if I could persuade her to get up. Maybe if she just felt my hand inside of hers she would know that I was there and take me for a walk.

The inexplicable urge to join her lingered in my mind for years. I did not completely understand where it was she went, but I knew life without her was that much more difficult. She was the random light in a drama-filled day.

I often reflect on her face when I want to feel beautiful. I hear Her words when I need that extra push. I feel Her presence when the tension is uneasy. I see Her eyes when I need to stay calm. I envision Her life when I need self-guidance. Though I doubt we are very much alike, I know I carry several of her traits.

When I want my daughter to feel loved, I take her out on walks. I bring fruit, activities and a small lesson to grasp later with practice. I make sure to hold her hand, kiss her face and listen to her recall her day. I try to bring that piece of heaven I experienced as a child to her whenever possible, even if I am feeling hellish. I will carry that piece of her with me forever. She showed me what love looks like. She awakened a confidence in me by walking in it herself.

Inspirational Writings
Carmen Patton

Sometimes I feel like I judge Her too harshly. I mean, she's struggling like so many other women do. Even though she sometimes thinks her struggle is unique, so many other women walk a similar walk. She talks about her walk with God, but her faith wavers like candlelight in a draft from time to time. Her walk doesn't always match her talk.

She seeks to lead a life that is pleasing to God. She's a woman after God's heart. Almost everyone that knows Her loves Her. People seek Her out for advice. She is an encourager and motivator for many. She has a kind heart and a sincere spirit. She loves hard and long. She's accomplished personally and professionally, yet she feels as if life is somehow passing her by.

Looking at Her, she seems to have it all together. She radiates beauty. She walks with her head held high, even when her spirits are low. She seeks to be confident yet humble. She exudes strength in her walk, in her talk, in her style, and the way she carries herself. Seemingly, she's comfortable in the skin she's in, yet she feels as if something is missing.

Though many find it hard to believe, within her lies a number of insecurities she's carried for years. She's flattered by the imitation of her by others. She is pursued by suitors. She lives a life that's picture-perfect for many. Yet no matter how many times she's told "I'm proud of you"; "You're beautiful"; "You inspire me," she still feels awkward and incomplete. Instead of feeling complete and whole, she feels alone and fragmented. She wishes she could do more, be more, have more, give more. She believes she's God's Daughter; sometimes she just feels He's forgotten or forsaken her.

I feel sorry for Her. Behind her beauty are the scars of putting her trust in the wrong people. Unrequited love has left her with emotional and physical baggage. Beneath her confidence is a blanket of shame and embarrassment for how foolishly she's lived at times. Underneath her strength is fear that God may never grant the desires of her heart.

I feel sorry for Her. If only she could see herself the way others do, she might feel differently. When she looks in the mirror, she sees someone who could be prettier if she didn't have the scars from the acne of her youth and the weight she carries from finding comfort and solace in food in her loneliest moments. She's surrounded by family and friends who love her, but she feels alone and incomplete, often because she's not a wife or a mother.

I feel sorry for Her. Her insecurities with who she is and isn't and what she has and doesn't have caused her to isolate herself from others. She has friendships on life support because her pride won't allow her to mend them. Despite the suitors she has, she can't build a meaningful relationship with a man because her past experiences won't allow her to trust anyone, including herself.

I feel sorry for Her. She's a Christian, yet instead of turning to God, she's often found temporary comfort in food and sex. She's regretfully used sex as an empowerment tool for herself. The closeness of sex makes her feel special and desired. The orgasmic euphoria is always short-lived for her though, and she's often left feeling empty and alone behind it.

I feel sorry for Her. Ironically, she can pinpoint when game is being run on everyone else, seemingly, except her. Well, sometimes she does know it's being run on her, but she's enjoying the fun times along the way, so she ignores the signs. She buries her head in the sand and thinks if she prays hard enough God will somehow bless that which He never ordained.

Despite the pity that I have for Her, sometimes she makes me so disappointed. She even angers me from time to time. It's hard to help Her though. She's extremely prideful. She likes to put on like she's together when she's unraveling piece by piece, day by day. Maybe you know someone like Her. You may even be someone like Her. I know Her well—better than most. You see, I am Her.

Inspirational Writings
Hope LeNoir

Because of my past, I'm destined to talk about how Her death lead me into deep depression. How I cut my wrists 14 times a week, smoked, I mean sniffed cocaine, and lost my virginity at eight. Then, I'm supposed to talk about the seven children I had and the three I lost before I was twenty-four years old. I forgot to mention I was a prostitute and a high school dropout six weeks before my graduation. Lord knows, given my past, I didn't complete my GED until I was 42 or even consider getting a college degree. It was her fault that she, my mother, died when I was seven months old, and I didn't and that's why my story should be the way it is. That would be normal for a woman like me. Normal for a woman with an abnormal past.

I think that's what I should write about, though I never talked to a psychologist about it.

Here is the reality. I'm not normal.

All that you just read about the "Her" I should have been, is normal. From what I read, normal isn't healthy. Neither is a lie. To this end, though I'm not normal, I was never diagnosed with depression, though I'm sure some devastating breakups in relationships took me there. I never slit my wrist, though I did cut myself the first time I tried to cut fabric for a homemade skirt. I confess, I've smoked, but not cocaine. Can you even smoke cocaine? I didn't sniff cocaine either, though I've heard every piece of money has some type of drug on it. I'll try sniffing money one day.

I never had children, though. I'd never considered having any. Is that bad? Is that a result of my past? I not only completed high school, but I have undergraduate and graduate degrees. Even more of the truth, my mother did die when I was an infant. I lived with an aunt who passed away when I was in grade school. More of the truth is that it was Her—my mom, my aunt, and other women in my life who allowed me to embrace the good things life has to offer.

It was all the Hers that I saw as one tribe of people who helped guide me, not distract me, to a greater avenue for spiritual, physical and mental bliss. It was Her who took me in and agreed to be my caretaker. It was Her who said, I'll take the baby now. It was Her who my aunt said,

"Don't go anywhere with anyone unless it's Her." It was Her who raised me after my mother died then Her mother died and said, "Now I'll raise her." Confused? Keep following.

It was her who said you're not watching television Monday through Thursday. It was Her who said, "every day, you'll sit at this table and you will do homework." It was Her who said if you don't cook, you'll wash every dish. And, well, I washed every dish.

It was Her who said dance, suck in your stomach, smile and sit up straight. I didn't want to be a basketball player, so I danced, sucked in my stomach, smiled and sat up straight. It was Her that enforced pride in my body and unskilled dance ability. It was Her who said, "Do it! Make the best decision for **you**. *I* can't make the decision for you." It was Her that said, "You decide" and "Don't sweat the small stuff in life."

It was Her who said Her dad's advice was "get some land." It was Her that reminded me that home is never too far away. It was Her who said "*That* Wonder Woman is gone, now *you* be Her. Go ahead and step out and fly." It was Her that took me all across the US and never stopped me when I wanted to glide across the oceans. It was Her that advised me to write down everything, I think, so everyone knows what I'm saying. It is Her that helps me make smarter decisions because she is my namesake. It is Her that teaches me to plan healthy meals. It is Her that hustles with class.

Now I am Her. I don't sweat the small stuff. I work hard and appreciate when I can play harder. I am Her, because I know my body is a temple and I must be healthy. I am Her because I love noise, and with noise, I feel safe. I am Her, because I take risks, appreciate risk, chances and mistakes which are a part of a growing life. I am Her because I have land for me, for my family, for peace. I am Her, because I told my nephew, I don't mind what you grow up to be. I don't mind if you're a can collector, but be the best at it and know I am never too far way. I am Her, because I told my niece, "If you don't need help getting dressed, that's okay. I'll be right here if you change your mind." And I sit, beside Her quietly, waiting in case she calls me to help. Why? Because I am Her. Never intruding. I am because I am the part of Her that is still alive. Because I am Her, I feel privileged. I feel beautiful. I feel wise. I feel covered. Brave. Strong. Beautiful. Conscious. Limitless in possibility. Strategic. Loving. Purposeful. I am Her, and so are you.

Inspirational Writings

Shoes

"The best way I can describe it is when you watch a movie you've seen already but still want the ending to change. Those shoes were the end of the movie."

-Ciera Shannon

Inspirational Writings
Rhonda Meydwell

I can't walk in heels. I truly cannot. Anything greater than a one-inch kitten heel or slight wedge, and I walk like Disney's Bambi attempting to cross ice for the first time. I don't bend my knees correctly, my ankles are wobbly, I look for something to hold onto, and eventually my foot slips out from under me, and before you know it I am all sprawled out on the ground. What's worse is that I am five foot, zero inches tall—I could use some elevation! So while many women can walk, dance, and run (how do they do that?) in heels, my short self typically sticks to flats (preferably the warm, furry kind). Until, for some reason, I decided I wanted to wear heels for my college graduation.

I did not start college until I was a few months' shy of turning forty. College was my lifelong dream, but, well, life was one of those things that kept postponing that dream. With the encouragement of my husband and family, I finally began my college experience. At the beginning of this journey, the road seemed long and arduous. I was certain it was going to take me a decade or more to accomplish earning a degree, after all, I was still working full time, and had a family with one child still at home. But, with hard work, determination, perseverance, and a LOT of support from my family and friends, four years later I was set to graduate Summa Cum Laude with a degree in English and Religious Studies from the University of Missouri. I was very proud of my accomplishment—very proud of myself. I felt I could do anything, so I decided I was going to walk across that stage in heels.

I have already mentioned that my family is one that provided constant encouragement and support as I worked through my courses. My husband and mom often read papers before I submitted them to professors, offering me helpful feedback and critique. Families have a way of keeping a person grounded, however, and mine is no exception. Even bigger news than I was graduating with honors, was news that I was planning to wear heels to accept my diploma. I didn't go crazy with my shoe selection, but I chose a patent nude sling-back with a peek-a-boo toe and a modest two-inch heel. Super cute, and I could adjust the sling-back to ensure good fit with less chance of the shoe slipping off the heel of my foot. Didn't matter—my family was soon laying odds at whether or not I would trip or fall in front of my entire graduating class at the commencement exercises. No one keeps you humble like your family.

I think God gives us a family for just that reason—not the only reason, maybe, but that is certainly part of the package. Humility, and those willing to help us to that end, is His protection. God says, "When pride comes, then comes disgrace, but with humility comes wisdom" (Prov 11:2). Believing as I do that God only wants good things for me, then giving me a sister who has video rolling hoping to catch the moment I sprawled out in front of the crowd, is a gift. The truth is, I *was* in danger of being prideful of my accomplishments. I was tempted to forget the Father who provided me with the opportunity, means, support, and love to accomplish anything. This piece of paper and bronze medallion had more to do with God pouring into my life and blessing me than it did anything I had cultivated within myself. Wearing heels, instead of flats, was the perfect reminder that when I choose to elevate myself, I run the very real risk of falling on my face. When I allow God to direct my steps, however, and "walk humbly with [my] God" (Micah 6:8), I am in constant reminder that all I have or accomplish is through Him, and I am thankful.

My graduation day was a very special one. Surrounded by family and friends who were so proud of me was fantastic. I shared my honor with them, because they truly kept me going when I was overwhelmed and thought I couldn't. As it turns out, I did not stumble throughout the convocation and commencement exercises, but I was mindful with each step I took that it was only He who kept me upright and nothing on my own.

Inspirational Writings
Demetria Adair

Ode to shoes, baby! I love shoes! I am drawn to them by a mystical magical power, no matter where I am. There is something about shoes and shopping for them that makes me as giddy as a teenage girl looking at her beau, longing to touch him.

I have gathered a nice collection and keep them like trophies in my closets. Each one in its own box, each box positioned outward with the picture or name of the shoe facing the front for easy access. Acquiring the many pairs I have has been an adventure and exhausting. There is a process for the shoe lover and shopper extraordinaire. The evolution of shoes is a phenomenon in itself: from leaves, tree twigs and animal skins to cover the feet to acrylic, glass, foam, and still more animal skins. Just as the production of shoes has evolved so has the practical purpose. No longer are shoes a primitive way to protect your feet from weather and land elements. Shoes are now a fashion statement that starts to speak before you open your mouth, an indicator of a person's life story.

Can we learn anything about a person based on the shoes they wear? Does the obsession for shoes some people have tell us anything about them? I think so. Have you ever heard someone compare how dog owners look like their dogs? Or that dog owners choose dogs with like personalities? Have you ever seen someone and looked at their shoes and said "that looks like them."? Shoes can depict social class, job classification, and personality.

When looking for the perfect pair of shoes, you don't walk in and pick the first beauty you see; no, you explore. Second you gather; you pick up the display and of course inquire about your size (or as close to your size as possible). Each time a pair is brought out you place them next to you until all styles are available. Third you try on; try them on, stand with them on, walk around with them on, look in the mirror with them on and ask others their opinions with them on. After the initial three steps you start imagining how the shoes will look with the perfect ensemble and what will people think of you when they see you? The process of elimination (or lack of elimination) and making choices (one color of one style, all colors of one style, multiple colors of many styles), strappies, pumps, slings, peek toe, wedges, stilettos; decisions, decisions, decisions, is the hardest thing to do and overwhelming just thinking about it!

A few weeks ago I was searching for a particular pair of shoes. Mentally I knew exactly where they were and visualized the color of the box and exactly what row in the closet they would be located. To my surprise they were not where I had thought, which made me dishevel all three of my closets looking for this one specific pair of shoes. As I was on the prowl I came across at least FOUR pair of brand spanking new shoes, still in the box, still in the plastic, still with the shoe shapers inside. I thought to myself, really Dee, really!

What does this one of many similar incidents say about me? It said mentally and physically I'm organized, but even in my meticulous organization I have too much going on. My obsession of shoes says about me that I like taking on things, I like gathering, organizing and showcasing what I have done. Wearing my different little trophies says I love the many abilities I have. I like for others to take note of those abilities.

My shoes tell an even bigger story about me. I'm usually in heels (pumps) which means I'm usually taking care of business. When I'm in sports shoes, I'm prepared to work harder. When I'm in flats (people are usually surprised), I'm ready for fun.

"Hello my name is Demetria and I am a shoeholic". Most compulsions have some logic and reason; the same is true about my shoes. Each pair tells a story or should I say, has a story associated with them. Each pair makes me feel different; they are a small biopic of me.

Inspirational Writings
Hiedi Emily

There are few things more instantly judged than shoes. Women either give a nod of approval for that cute pair of pumps sported by the lady at the office or a slight wince of secret jealousy. In a society where a red sole has become a status symbol for men, as well as, women, what is the "right way" to objectively observe the single most talked about accessory trend of the century? Is there something more beneath the soul's choice of soles?

I believe there is. All of you fashionistas reading can put your stiletto clad feet up knowing these observations are made by a lady who is the happy owner of over 60 pairs of the cutest, most amazing 5" platform pumps, booties, espadrilles, and boots. They range in deliciously fabulous colors and patterns. More importantly, I hope it changes the way you view some less fashionable shoe choices, and the precious people who wear them.

- *Dirty, worn boots, male size 10* - A hard working blue collar man wears them. In Texas that could be a bona fide cowboy instead of a construction worker. He's glad that they're broken in, and has no interest in a new pair. His goal is not to impress, but to get the job done. He works hard to take care of his family because he loves them. This ragged pair of boots, that probably should have been replaced a year ago, (in fact his wife has secretly thought of throwing them out) for him is a badge of honor, and may be the only way he knows how to express that love.

- *Clean, gently loved, black kitten heel pumps* - This lady plays it safe. She can wear them with a dress, suit, or slacks. She keeps them at her desk, just in case a meeting pops up unexpectedly. Absolutely no thought is required, and no worries about them being "too feminine" for the office. After all, even though it's the 21st century, in corporate life whether truly existing in her office or only in the insecurity of her mind, she and too many women like her believe showing their femininity in the workplace is taboo. That it impedes advancement to highlight our differences. This woman carries too much - too much stress, too much guilt, too much on her calendar every week. When she's at work she feels guilty that she's not doing more with her family. When she leaves close to on time she wonders if she's done enough to be considered for the upcoming promotion. If she was truthful, while she needs the money, it's a job she doesn't truly want. If money wasn't so tight, the truth is, she'd rather be home with her family. She'd rather step out and give the dream of her own business or ministry a test spin. She keeps sacrificing hoping someday things will be different.

- *Vivid color tennis shoes* - This person is more concerned about the statement than the cost. You will find him strutting like a peacock at the gym, but rarely do you actually see him working out. You can't get them dirty, you know! There is one exception to this I've observed. The basketball lover! He will jump into a pickup game at every opportunity. His love for the game, and how he feels slam dunking the ball, or out maneuvering his opponent, stealing the ball right out of his hand overrides the need to keep his high tops pristine. On the court he has joy. He is free. He may be slightly slower than back in school, but he does his best to ignore reality. It's worth it because on the court things make sense. No surprises, no pressure, no disappointments: just friends, trash talk, and the game!

- *Cheap flip flops* - In America they are usually relegated to the gym shower, or maybe the beach. However, in Belize they represent two key functions. Firstly, most of the children don't have shoes. This leaves them susceptible to bites and disease. Shoes are a protection. Secondly, they're a booming enterprise for clever children! I witnessed this first hand during a mission trip in Independence Village. Children came from everywhere for the precious flip flops. We were surrounded! After a while, one of our guides told us we need to pay better attention because we had given over three pairs each to a handful of boys. They would run to their shack, hide them, and come back for more. She explained that after we leave the boys go downtown and sell them for as much as they can. Three or four pairs could get them enough to buy rice and beans for a week. Most children there have only parent with no job or one that pays so little they can't feed their kids on a daily basis. A week of groceries paid for is a big deal! Even though we had to turn them down when they returned for round two, I have to admit, I was proud of them and impressed with their entrepreneurial ingenuity. They would rather sell than beg.

Inspirational Writings
Hope LeNoir

The most fascinating pair of shoes I saw were on President Obama's feet. There was a photo of him in a magazine, sitting on a couch with his feet up on a table. He was reading. His suit fit well. It was nice and dark. The tops of his shoes were shining, like they were created three minutes prior to me turning to that page. The soles, however, were worn. That meant a lot. His shoes tell me he is a man who cares about the way he looks and how he makes people feel when he walks in the room. His shoes also tell the story of a hard worker, mentally and physically. The worn bottoms tell me he is well grounded. That day I saw him in the magazine, I respected him even more.

I have shoes worthy of that same kind of respect. The gold heeled shoes I was wearing when my car stopped working in Louisiana. The same gold heels I wore when I lost my job in Texas. I wore them again while strutting down the career-fair aisle. Those gold heeled shoes were the same shoes I wore as I walked down the street to a church I'd never visited before. Those were the shoes that fit my size-12 feet. Those were the shoes my aunt, now battling dementia, bought me when I was 17 years old. Those were the shoes that shined and were surprisingly comfortable.

I didn't like those shoes, because they were too mature for me. But, those were the shoes that allowed me to walk to church and still look good. They were shoes that attracted the interviewer to me. They were the shoes that got me the job, a not so simple pair of shoes.

Shoes have complex meaning. Since I've reflected on my gold heeled shoe journey, I always expected shoes to be meaningful. They should be nice, but worn on the sole. They represent your role, your purpose and your journey. For example, kids want to wear them because of what they represent or who they represent. Pumped shoes may mean adulthood. Loafers are a sign of strength, intelligence and comfortably. At least they were. Converse represented confidence, but cost effective, smart style. I had every color of size-12 converse a teenager could find. As an adult, confident, bold, cute AND no toe exposure are what Converse mean to me.

People tend to shoes according to their meaning, too. For example, children and adults may toss them on the floor or they may line them up against the door or in the closet just so. This could represent an intent of cleanliness, holiness, respect for convenience. Some leave their shoes in the trunk because what they mean outside the doors of their home mean more than what they mean inside their home.

Today the shoes I wear mean I care. I care about myself. I care about the people who are in the room with me or looking at me in a photo. I care about the little child that can't wait to be in my Shoes.

Now, there are no crunched up toes for my size 12 feet. I learned to find comfy shoes that don't hurt my nails or bend my toes. No pointy toed shoes for me, either. They are nice, but painful. No wide shoes. My ankles are narrow, my toes are long. Yes, I still wear and love pumps and what they represent. I love the moment I discovered some are more comfortable. Shoes with heels, bring with them some boss calves and a small hump to the behind that's not really there.

Shoes. They say a lot whether you wear them or not. His shoes: mature, not mature, sexy, established, bold, still growing, sometimes ambitious, appreciative of God's gift, then sometimes lost or conflicting of personality. Her shoes: mature, fun, proactive, calf toning, thankful, caring, naïve, contradictory. They mean and represent a lot, no matter where you wear them. They touch a lot of people, young or seasoned.

Inspirational Writings
Carmen Patton

His Shoes
When I was a kid, I thought my Daddy had the biggest feet in the world. You know, giant-like big. Right now, his shoes will swallow my feet, and I've got a pretty big foot for a woman. My Daddy is right around 6'4". So, literally, I don't personally know very many people that can fit his shoes. Figuratively, I don't personally know that many people that can fit his shoes either.

My Daddy, as giant-like as he is, is as gentle as a lamb, especially when it comes to his girls. He's been a husband almost 43 years. He's been a father almost 39 of those years. I've never seen his shoes walk towards my mother or my sister and me in a threatening way. I've never seen his shoes leave our home without returning. I've never seen his shoes sitting idly.

My Daddy's shoes were stable and sturdy. So is he. He is faithful in our church. He's a good husband to my mother. He's a good father to my sister and me. My Daddy wore the shoes of a hard worker. He is a provider; he is financially secure. Growing up he sacrificed a lot of time with us, but we always knew where he was. The man in those shoes worked many a 16 hour shift before he retired. The man in those shoes consistently kept a roof over our head with cars in the driveway. The man in those shoes took us on family vacations. The man in those shoes bought me and my sister our first cars. The man in those shoes paid college tuition. I've been out on my own over 16 years, but I can still count on the man in those shoes for anything.

Naturally, I expect a lot from a man. The first man that I ever loved and that ever loved me has tried his best to give me nothing but the best. Whatever we needed, he made sure we had. Whatever we wanted (within reason), we had. I don't look for a man to be my Daddy. I have a Daddy. Arguably, I actually have one of the best daddies as daddies go. I pray that God will send me a husband like Daddy, but no man could ever fill Daddy's shoes in my book.

Her Shoes
Like most little girls, I used to try on my Mama's shoes. Mama doesn't have feet like Daddy. She barely stands 5'4". Everyone in our home was taller than her. So, I could literally wear her shoes by the time that I was like 13 or 14 years old. Figuratively, though, I'll never be able to fill her shoes.

My Mama is the product of a single parent home. She's a strong woman raised by a strong woman. She's my example of a Proverbs 31 woman. She's a faithful wife, a doting mother, and a loyal friend. The one thing that will dig in her craw every time and bring her Mama Bear claws out though is if you mess with the Daddy Bear or the baby girl bears. Nobody, I mean absolutely nobody, messes with Mama's "girls."

My Mama's shoes were comfortable and practical because Mama was busy wearing many hats. Mama was a teacher. Mama was a Girl Scout Leader. Mama was the first person to lead Children's Church at our church. I call her the Baby Whisperer because nobody can rock a baby to sleep faster than my Mama. Mama loves children. She's influenced a countless number of children in our church, on her job, and in our community.

I watched my mother take care of her grandmother and her mother until their deaths. I've watched my mother visit the sick and shut in. I've watched her take care of friends while they've been ill or recovering. The care and concern she shows for others is admirable. Her strength is astounding.

My Mama woke up before the light of day and went to bed at the darkest of night often. She laid out breakfast in the morning, packed lunches, taught children, came home and fixed dinner, helped with homework, graded papers, and miscellaneous small things that help a household run five days a week. On the weekends, she was a Girl Scout Leader, an errand runner for senior citizens, and a youth leader in our church. She did all of those things well. I can barely get anywhere on time, cook a decent meal or keep my house tidy, and I'm just one person. I have nowhere near the responsibilities my Mama did at my age. I tell her all the time, "Mama, I don't know how you did it!"

When I was that little girl standing in Mama's shoes, even though they fit my feet, I never realized how big they were. I may be able to wear Mama's shoes, but I may never be able to fill Mama's shoes. And I'm okay with that because it gives me something better to strive for every day.

Inspirational Writings
Ciera Shannon

Most mornings I would watch her get ready.

She would have the electric curlers plugged into the front of the mirror. Her clothes, badge, and other necessities were spread across her bed. She moved quickly, and every few minutes or so glanced over at the clock.

"There's food in the fridge," she'd remind me. "And be nice to your brother and sister."

"How long you gonna be at work?" I would ask.

"I'll be back as soon as I can." She always said that.

She went on to bathe, make lunch and then it was time. I knew she went to work every day, but it was always finalized when she pulled out the black flats. They weren't anything fancy, just a casual pair of kicks. But pulling them out made her leaving official. The best way I can describe how I felt when I saw those black flats is when you watch a movie you've seen already, but still want the ending to change but you know it's already set in stone. Those shoes were the end of the movie. They brought closure to the inevitable final scene.

I knew my mom had to do what was necessary for us to survive so I did my best not to complain as much. I would help her with her things or do whatever was asked to make the morning go more smooth, but I refused to help with anything that had to do with those shoes.

If they were misplaced I was of no assistance. I would move slow if she asked me to bring them to her. I even went so far as to hide them one time, but they were replaced with another black replica. Helping with them would mean I was ok with her leaving. Helping with them would mean I didn't mind.

The truth is, I did mind, because I missed my Mommy. I wanted to spend time with her, talk to her about nothing, or just sit in a room with her. Some days, I would have a full blown attitude, and I am sure she had no idea why. I was upset, because I knew I was going yet another day without my Mommy. I knew I was about to spend another day watching the clock and counting down to the last seconds she would arrive.

I eventually learned to get over myself. That too was another lesson in life. I began to intentionally help out more in whatever area possible. I would fuss at my siblings about keeping the house clean so she could relax when she got home. I would try to give her space when she made it home after a long day. I even tried to get her clothes ready for her one day, but that was an epic fail so I left that to her.

I didn't fully understand, at the time, the sacrifices my Mom made for our family, but I appreciate her so much for them now. She could have easily allowed life to get the best of her but she didn't and I couldn't be more proud. I remember those black flats and how at one point they were the bane of my existence. Now I view them as an example of love and sacrifice.

Inspirational Writings
DiAnne Malone

It was the third week of class, and they still had no books.

Okay, only 15 out of 19 had no books, but when I tell you those 15 had on some boss shoes! What?!

I walk around the room slowly and case the 30 feet I'm there to serve. Eighteen, nineteen-year-old brown children, sitting in desks, at an HBCU, in the heart of the most impoverished part of Memphis, wearing $200 pairs of shoes, and carrying no books ($96). A memory is evoked.

My uncle, black as coal, teeth bright white, a gray streak of hair shooting down at almost the center of his head, like a two-way tarred road split down the middle by a thick white line. He is talking to me while chewing on his pipe. He is reclined. His shoes are expensive. He begins his pontification with the same four words.

"You know one thang?" I sigh, but not loud enough for him to hear. I am 19 and uninterested in the words of any person over 30.

"Sir?"

"You can tell a lot about a negro by looking at his shoes. If he's got on a cheap pair of shoes, he probably ain't worth shit…"

My uncle is a retired principle. He'd seen lots of shoes. Middle Schooler shoes. Teacher shoes. Parent shoes. He is also a bail bondsman. Imagine the shoes.

"Don't you let me catch you walking out of the house with a raggedy pair of shoes on your feet. If I can't get you nothing else, I can keep you in some shoes."

"Yessir," I say. I giggle behind a smile made perfect by braces.

"And get your lesson." He says.

"Yessir," I say.

My sister would wear her worse pair of shoes around my uncle, just so he could buy her three new pairs to replace the old ones. My cousin did the same with her father. It became an obsession of ours. How can we get new shoes?

Times have changed. Since teaching at university, I have become disillusioned with shoes, especially when shoes come before learning, before thinking, before creating, before writing, understanding, and changing the world.

In the classroom, my rant begins with shoes, because someone paid for the shoes my students wear. They paid hundreds of dollars for a jump man logo or the letters M and K strategically placed together. They, too, taught their children that presentation of the feet was important, but neglected to say presentation of the mind is more important.

"Get your lesson," is my closing exclaim. "And don't come in here with fancy shoes, unless you have a book in your hand." I extend my index finger, my arm. I lock my elbow. I sweep my arm around the room. "And I mean that." I want to put it on my syllabus, but I know that is extreme. It goes too far. There will be time for too far, later on in the semester.

But they don't get it, not yet. It takes three more weeks, several F's at mid-term, the threat of losing financial aid. The unscrupulous red markings on the bright white paper, all across the masterpieces they'd banged out on their shiny laptops only four hours prior.

It takes humiliation. Yes. I humiliate. It takes them tracking their poverty through a narrative essay. It takes a descriptive essay about the first time they saw their father smoke crack.

It takes understanding that this school is not the same school some of their parents attended. It takes two-parent home kids seeing that kids from the "mound" only have one parent, or no parent. These kids reconsider their choice for higher ed. They consider themselves better than the other kids. They are not better.

Inspirational Writings

One kid scoffed when I asked about his parents. He looked at me, as if I was the greenest, silliest woman he'd ever seen. He answered, "Professor Malone, the streets are my parents." He meant it. He meant it when he got expelled for brandishing a weapon at a school sponsored party. He meant it when he got shot in the back twice while on campus during a Labor Day barbecue. It took that for me to understand the importance of their shoes, and it took me demanding a book and a pen and paper and an essay to get them to understand how vital it is that they pick up a book, read it, write through their unique circumstances, and grow through the ink from their pen.

A week after midterms, I take attendance. "Say here, and hold your book up in the air, please." I call each name and look up from my attendance roster, over my trendy glasses, to see each student grin and say, "I got mine, Professor Malone." I drop my head so they won't see me smile. "…AND, I got my J's on," a young man in the back says. The students laugh. I indulge them.

"I see you, pimp'n." I say.

I see you.

Anger

"The best thing that comes out of righteous anger is holy action."

Hiedi Emily

Inspirational Writings
Hope Lenoir

I absolutely understand anger. I am aware that anger hurts my soul and damages my physical health. Though it sometimes gives me credibility when exposed, I *really* don't embrace the value of acknowledging or holding on to too much anger, especially when I can think of all the other things I could be doing. It wasn't until I was well past my thirties that I even recognized when I was angry myself or understood when I should be angry.

Most connotations about anger are negative. It doesn't have to be that way. There is a positive. Knowing what you're angry about is super important. Knowing what you're feeling can reveal what is important. Robust knowledge about your anger paves the way to smarter decisions, and, though sometimes hurtful or sometimes enlightening, an abundance of awareness about yourself. It can cause you to pause and think more rationally. To this end, experiencing anger, believe it or not, can be healthy when kept under control.

As a career coach, I've learned the importance of expressing how I feel when I'm angry. I have an illness that often influences how I acknowledge my feelings. The good news is, I am now more aware of how I feel, and more importantly, why I feel a certain way. For example, one day an employee made a racist remark to me at work. The average person would have been extremely angry. I, on the other hand, ignored it. Once a colleague found out, he brought my behavior to my attention. He let me know this wasn't something I should hold in. It's something I should address with the person talking to me. The "aha" moment came when he explained, "Think of all the other people this would affect in the future if you don't say anything. This could make others extremely angry."

From that moment on, I got out of the "I'll get over situations like this" mode or the "That really didn't make me angry" mode to, "I have to acknowledge this behavior could invoke anger. I have to do and say something about what makes me angry and how we all can move forward." Because of this incident, many people—me, the initiator and the people in the future--could be affected socially. This means, it isn't healthy to hold on to or avoid resolution when you are angry about something. Of course the situation affects you and your health, but the situation also has the potential to effect the health of others. Be aware of this effect and do the right thing about it.

I've also learned how important this concept is for both my mental and physical health to not hold in anger. We all know that holding anger can cause stress, and anxiety attacks. Research also tells us that repressing anger can cause heart disease. These are things that can be avoided by simply acknowledging and appropriately addressing the core issues.

Exploding in anger may not be the best approach either. The reality is, exploding out of anger doesn't always get rid of the feeling of anger. On top of that, this behavior is bad for the heart as well. Last, but not least, know that some reasons for anger can be trivial, and the expression of anger can be small.

In all relationships, both professional and personal, be careful what you say and what you do when angry. Think about how the outcome will affect you and those around you. Start by acknowledging your anger. Some ways to get rid of anger is to seek to understand the situation. This my favorite approach. It means, reach out to those involved, pray or meditate and get help from a knowledgeable and trustworthy individual. Going for a walk or run, may also be helpful. Sometimes the resolution is to simply change the environment that causes you stress. This could mean adding a lamp, or avoiding that grocery store in particular, or even changing jobs. Knowing how to quickly get over anger in a positive way will improve your quality of life. Start by understanding why you feel angry. Seek to understand the reason the situation happened. Choose a healthy way to resolve the anger and move on to a healthier, happier place for you and all those involved.

Inspirational Writings
Hiedi Emily

I didn't grow up in a Christian home. My dad died before I was two and my mom suffered from mental illness. I had four older brothers who had their own problems. I was the baby and only girl and had to keep it together. It was organically conveyed to me that my role was to be nice, make peace, and not dare to have my own opinion. After being abused by my step-father and seeing that my mom's reaction to that knowledge was that it was my fault, I had no fight. Any anger that I had a righteous right to was shoved so far down inside me that I became a compliant sycophant for anyone who gained access to my life.

Normal, nice girls, don't get angry.

It's a prevalent concept in the church and the world. I've heard messages in church that have left me with the impression that if I was angry, I was most likely impatient, and since patience is a fruit of the Holy Spirit, my emotions were in the way of being properly Spirit-filled. Psalms says, if you have great peace you won't be offended. I have often felt manipulated by others who have used these verses to make me feel, if I hotly disagreed with them, I was sinning. Even the world addresses anger through a special therapy that tells us that anger has to be "managed." These sessions are designed to lead people away from anger, leaving them with a feeling of shame. Mad is bad.

Comic books have actually done a better job at addressing anger than most self-help books on taming anger. A hero - not a villain – was created to give us an image for anger. You know the big green guy I'm talking about. The one who says, "Don't make me angry. You wouldn't like me when I'm angry." So, now, are we unlikeable if we get angry? If I want to be liked and accepted, I should never be angered.

I came to know Jesus as my Savior right before my thirteenth birthday. I heard the same things in my church. Polite, good Christian girls didn't make waves. After all, doesn't the Bible say women are to be silent in church? Since I didn't grow up in church or any form of Christendom, I didn't know there was anything else. I thought the way they showed me what a sanctified Christian woman looked like, talked like, and acted like was all there was. All of this kept me in a wounded vulnerable state which made me ripe for being spotted by predators. I wound up in a very abusive marriage where any semblance of self-esteem was completely destroyed.

Abuse in my life was obviously cyclic, but what if, when I was little, someone had been there to teach me what I know now about anger? What if someone had told me, it's okay to be angry? God gets angry. The Bible tells us in Ephesians to be angry, but sin not. This simple verse has amazing freedom in it! It is saying you can be angry, and it's not automatically a sin!

There are more than a few healthy reasons to be angry, and I'm angry about them! Abuse and injustice angers me. The devil's schemes anger me. Greed and injuries to others, crime, poverty, famine, deadly illness, and exploitation all anger me. Sometimes I am so angry that I feel hot in my body. Sometimes I cry. *The best thing that comes out of this kind of righteous anger is holy action.*

How many children die from measles, the black plague, or the flu today? The question sounds kind of silly in 2016. But, do you know why the plague is gone? Someone got angry. One day some mom, some dad, some doctor or nurse held the umpteenth dead child in their arms and declared they had had enough. They got hopping mad! They declared, "if I can help it, no more kids will die from this! It seems impossible; it looks hopeless. Yet, I will make a way where there is no way!" Throughout history, you will discover that many of those way-makers were of the faith.

This applies to so many things. The kid on the playground that won't let the school bully push that tiny kid in class anymore is an angry hero. Harriet Tubman, along with all of us in the present day anti-slavery fight to end human trafficking, are angry heroes. Godly women who are sick and tired of the devil lying to our kids, attacking our marriages, families, churches, and country with his wicked schemes better rise up and be angry heroes!

We need to get our warrior princess on and take that anger to the very throne room of God boldly crying out for the justice, deliverance, and protection we need. Ladies, our world is at stake. Too often it seems like the gates of hell are prevailing instead of God's kingdom storming those gates and destroying them to let the captives go free. It was once said all that is needed for evil to triumph is for good men to do nothing. Let it be said of us that in our day, in our Esther moment,

Inspirational Writings

we stood, "in such a times as this." Allow righteous anger to be the fuel that the Holy Spirit uses to embolden us to make a difference!

7 Women 7 Words

Inspirational Writings
Ciera Shannon

As adults, when something is off, internally, we instinctively know to remove ourselves from the alarming situation. Imagine, as a child, understanding you had no power to remove yourself from that situation. You had no control over what is done to your body or what words are spoken to and around you. Many of us would like to think we would know how to react. We say things like, *that couldn't have been me*. Or, *I would have said something*. My "so-and-so" taught me to speak up, not realizing that not all have a "so-and-so" who was able to teach such strength.

I will admit anger is all I knew at one point. Especially when I realized that my normal was not normal. My pain was, in fact, real. For a while I could not feel anything without anger being attached to it. In my eyes, people were selfish, everyone had a motive, no good deed was without payment, and my life, upon escaping, became a mental hell all over again. I could not enjoy any moment without adding a negative. When good things happened to me I would sabotage them almost immediately. I did not feel I was worthy of happiness. To me happiness wasn't real, but anger was.

I often reflect on the things I endured and the truth is, unfortunately I had not managed to move past them. The screaming, the fighting, the encounters with pedophiles. Questions such as what exactly should the response be from a six-year-old to a man demanding to kiss her, or the fourteen-year-old to the drunken man asking to have her, and her being blamed for him asking? What is the course of action when you know your mother cannot protect you because she cannot protect herself? How can you get away when you know your friend is being sexually abused by the man who adopted her—and that man uses her to ask you to reveal your privates to him?

I was meek and timid. I was a child! My every action went towards the acceptance of others. I would dance, fight, even lie upon request. My personality was silenced by violence. My laugh limited with worry. Fear became first nature. Despite my ability to feed and clean myself, I knew I was a dependent. I knew that this particular environment was my safe haven.

I was not guaranteed a peaceful setting in another home, so I stayed silent. I watched and observed what became my normal. I adapted to the unpredictable space and tip-toed around the aggressor, the predator and the enablers. Everyone knows but everyone is silent. The unspoken admonition is to keep your head down and just be thankful that your situation isn't that bad. Family is family and we're all we got.

Is that really enough? Why are we encouraged to settle because someone happens to have the same DNA as us? Why is it considered taboo when we remove ourselves permanently from any type of abuse, when the abuse is coming from a family member? Are we not worthy of respect?

Anger validated my pain and soothed my yearning for respect. It gave truth to the unforgivable flaws. I was not perfect, but anger filled the void. And, then, one day I woke up feeling drained and completely dead inside. My husband was on his way to work. My daughter, optimistic and full of life had written out her entire day on her chalk board. Number one: "hug Mommy and give her a kiss."

My son awakened and was calling my name the best way he knew how. One sock on and the other in the world of lost socks. He was smiling and reaching for me and talking in a language only he understands. I picked him up and rubbed his back like I do every morning. I kissed his cheeks and rubbed my fingers through his hair, a routine I had developed without noticing until recently.

That day I realized I was no longer in that consuming place of anger anymore. I could let go and allow love to fill my being. My family was right here, and they were waiting for me with kisses, hugs, letters with misspelled words and conversations about our dreams. From that day forward, I no longer gave my past permission to invade my thoughts or persuade my emotions in a way that would disrupt my day. I acknowledge the wrongdoings and I move forward with what I have in front of me. Those who have wronged me in whatever way have been forgiven and placed in my life accordingly. I will not judge them because of their past but I will acknowledge their actions in the present.

Inspirational Writings
Rhonda Maydwell

Anger, in its rawest form, tends to bring out the worst in us. Case in point, in my teenage full-of-drama years, I was a fan of Marilyn Monroe. I had several posters of the beautiful woman in my bedroom and one on the outside of my bedroom door so she greeted me every time I entered. My sister and I rarely argued (honestly), but one Saturday afternoon while our parents were gone, we had the sister fight to end all sister fights.

At one point my little sister followed me to my room, I slammed the door in her face, and what happened next would prove to be the greatest Baker family controversy of all time… I heard the life size poster on my door rip in half. I flung open my door to see a legless Marilyn looking at me, while the bottom half of the poster dragged along the fawn colored carpet. I could not even see straight (did I mention full-on teen drama mode?). Before I could put together a coherent thought, I screamed, "You have killed her all over again!!!" I am not even kidding—I really did. Now, this story is told at *every* family gathering and to any new person who finds their way into our clan. It brings belly laughs and streaming tears with every telling… At the time, however, this was no laughing matter.

To this day my sister, who cried an apology for at least an hour, promises the rip was an accident. I am dubious. She claims that her hand was outstretched, and it was *my* slamming of the door that caused her hand to catch the poster and rip it. Uh, huh…tell it to the judge.

The part that I *abhor* in this story, however, is the full knowledge that I was completely out of control during my rage. In hindsight, it was such a trivial matter (you know, we cannot even remember what we were arguing about to begin with), yet I was consumed with anger and wanted to destroy my baby sister. In Ephesians, the Bible exhorts, "In your anger, do not sin" (4:26). The older I get, I question if it is possible for me to be angry and not sin.

In church we learn that only "righteous anger" such as that displayed by Jesus when He overturned the tables in the Temple is not sinful…but, honestly, I don't think I ever pull off righteous anger. Even if I have a cause that might live up to righteous anger material, I dirty it up with judgmental and condemning thoughts. I am not capable of saying, "You have turned my

Father's house into a den of thieves," without adding, "you dumb jerks, enjoy your stay in Hell!" Just me? Clearly I still have room for growth in this area.

Anger may often lead to sin, but this does not mean that we bottle up our feelings or deny our emotions. It also does not mean that we do not strive to right wrongs and correct injustices when we have that opportunity. As women, we are often inclined (and pushed) to do just that. Bottled anger ferments into bitterness, and bitterness rots a person from the inside out. Anger and bitterness rob a person of peace and joy. It is this angry or bitter state of being that I try to eliminate from my life. The best antidote I know for banishing anger and bitterness from my life is extending forgiveness to the one who has offended.

Forgiveness is nearly impossible to cultivate on one's own. Let's be honest, forgiveness just is not in most people's nature. Forgiveness does not tell the perpetrator that what he or she has done is okay. Instead, forgiveness releases the offended one from the enslaving power of anger and bitterness. When I am consumed by an injustice done against me, I cannot sleep, eat, or effectively complete my duties. I become anxious and my body is tense—I may even have a headache. I literally allow my anger to make me sick. Forgiveness loses the shackles that join me to the one who hurt me. It doesn't let the offender off the hook, I set myself free. Jesus offered forgiveness to those whose very sins nailed him to his cross, and that is the example that I try to follow.

In my experience, practicing forgiveness can only be done through prayer and Bible study. Like a good strong tea, we must steep ourselves in the Word that reminds us of the amazing grace and forgiveness bestowed upon us by a Father who gave His son for wretches like us. Ask God for patience, wisdom, joy, and peace (all things we cannot access on our own when we are angry). It isn't easy, but it is grace and forgiveness that often makes us look different and becoming to non-believers. I wish I could report that I have kicked the anger bucket completely to the curb, but I would be dishonest if I did. It is a daily struggle, and when I fail, it is God's grace to me that guides me back to forgiveness and grace towards others, and that seems right.

Inspirational Writings
Carmen Patton

You probably don't even remember what you were doing August 11, 2013. You likely don't know what day of the week it was. It was a Sunday.

I got up that morning and got dressed in a special dress that I'd ordered for that day. August 11 is the day I was born. It was my 36th birthday. I was feeling myself that day. I felt good. I'd been maintaining a 120-pound weight loss, and I was headed to praise the Lord for the good things He had done. Nothing could go wrong that day. It was my birthday, and God knew how I felt about the day He gave me life. My birthday was the one day a year that everything went my way. That is until August 11, 2013.

Everything happened so fast that day. Really, everything happened so fast that weekend. My godfather had been hospitalized almost three weeks before. Life was going to change for him, but that Thursday we learned he'd be released soon. He was doing well. God had come through once again. Prayer works. God had showed up and out once again.

The day that he got his good report, I missed visiting him. He had encouraged me to not let him being in the hospital interrupt my exercise routine. So, that Thursday, I worked out. I'd see him Friday when I got out of the beauty salon. When I got there that Friday, he was sicker than I'd ever seen him. I trust God though; so, this was just the devil trying to sneak in and get some of God's glory. Never did I think that the conversation that we had that Friday would be the last conversation we would ever have. Never did I think that would be the last time that I saw him alive.

I believed God for a turnaround. I believed God for a breakthrough. I believed God to be a healer. We were all praying. His youngest daughter had insisted each visitor write a Bible verse, and then she'd hang them in the room. The walls in his room were covered in Bible verses, surrounded with God's Word. There was no way the devil in hell was going to win. My godfather knew God for himself. I wasn't worried about his soul. I knew his soul was safe whenever God called for him, but I never thought he was going to call for him so soon.

As I sat in the cold hospital waiting room in my birthday dress on my birthday, I didn't think God would call for him that day. He'd been in my life from day one. He was closer than a friend to my parents; he was their brother. His wife and my mother have been friends since they were 10 years old. His daughters are like my little sisters. He was like another father for me. Other than my father and my pastor, he was one of the most influential men in my life. So, yes, I grieved his transition. Yet, I had a great deal of anger in me at the same time. One of the most influential people in my life had gone to Heaven, and I wasn't just sad. I was filled with anger.

I was angry at myself that I'd gone to exercise instead of going to the hospital that Thursday. I was angry that my last memory of him kept trying to take the place of so many good memories. I was angry because he and his wife were supposed to go on retired people trips with my parents. I was angry because he hadn't walked his daughters down the aisle or seen them have children. I was angry because nothing bad is supposed to happen on my birthday. I was angry because I am a Christian, and I saw someone I loved who was saved getting his heavenly pay day and I was selfish enough to be mad about it.

I spent a great deal of time harboring anger about my godfather's death. I had questions. I eventually came to terms with the fact that a lot of the anger that I had towards my godfather's death was directed towards God. I even had the unmitigated gall to tell Him so.

God why couldn't he get his three score and ten? Why did my godmother have to become a widow? Why did his sister have to lose her brother and closest friend? Why did disease have to invade his body? Why did his daughters have to lose their father? How will I ever feel right celebrating my birthday when a person that I loved dearly transitioned on that day?

I asked God all those questions. I spent days and nights in tears and prayer. God took one of the most painful situations of my life and allowed me to get closer to Him. I couldn't talk to anyone but Him about these things. Everyone else near and dear to me was also near and dear to my godfather, so they had their own questions and issues to work through.

I had to become more intimate with God through this. That was the only way that I could get over the anger. He's still working with me on the pain. I still shed tears over my godfather. I still grieve him often. I'm no longer bitter though. I'm no longer filled with anger. I still feel God could have worked that situation out any number of ways that would have been a better outcome in my eyes. He didn't though, and day by day I'm coming to terms with that.

Inspirational Writings
DiAnne Malone

As far back as I can remember, I stuffed down anger, like pushing garbage into an overrun trash can.

No, it was more like throwing stuff into a closet stacked to the hilt with junk. I shoved the new anger on top of the old anger and quickly closed the door to keep all the anger, past and present, from spilling out.

I learned to do this as a child during a time I was angry about a lot of things. In retrospect, I was angry most of the time. I was angry about things I couldn't control, and even more angry that no one asked why I was angry in the first place. Because no one ever asked, I never told, and thus came to the conclusion, since anger wasn't a discussion to be had with me, it was bad for me.

Anger is not bad for me. Not expressing my anger is bad for me. Just like the sitcom scene when there is too much in the closet, there came a time I'd open the door to drop in a feather weight bit of anger, and the entire mess would come crashing down. This is when I would explode.

Most people don't believe I have a bad temper. Most people who know me fairly well would say I am the most laid back person they've met. I get compliments on how relaxed and chill I seem. My husband brags on me all the time, because I don't nag and make drama for him. My children know, "when mom's calm, there are about to be some consequences and repercussions." Chill is what I *do*, but I'm certain it is not who I *am*.

When things make me angry, I simmer and seethe. That's not healthy; at least that's what people say. It wasn't until I saw a great little film called, "Inside Out," that I discovered that anger is not a bad thing. Anger does have its place, and it keeps us healthy if we use it to empty our emotional trashcans.

Anger allows us the opportunity to release all of those bad emotions, feelings, disappointments, heartbreaks and aches. Now, I get it. I get it that God wants us to be able to release those strong feelings so that we won't bottle them up and do more damage than good. He doesn't desire that the bottle explodes leaving the shards of cutting anger to injure the innocent that might be standing by. Explosion is not the intent of anger. It's quite the opposite. Healthy anger allows us to heal. Anger, if handled with care, is meant to cleanse us, to give us an opportunity to move toward rational decisions. Without the perversion of sin, anger is a blessing.

I prefer sitting with that anger, now that I know it's not bad. But I can't sit with it forever. Trash stinks. I have to take it out sometime. Empty the bin and refill as needed. Clean out the closet of anger. Throw away the refuse. Vacuum the bits of debris. Purge the stuff that's too small, the problems that are too big. Take it to God's curb; leave it there. Replace my weaknesses for God's strength.

With the bins clean and refilled with God's grace, I am experiencing the blessing of trolling my challenges for anger triggers. It is a beautiful anger-filled work in progress to be given permission by the One who created me to feel anger. It is a gift to know that anger, if handled with care, can grow me into a more peaceful and useful person.

Inspirational Writings
Demetria Bowers-Adair

Not to wear a pseudo hallo, but I take pride in the fact that, generally speaking, I am slow to anger. Maybe because I'm pretty transparent, and I don't allow buildup of resentment or hurtful issues that may plant seeds of anger. Most of the time I don't sugar coat (I am tactful), and I shoot straight from the hip. Get it out. Talk about it. Move forward. However, there was a time when I would let things brew, hold on to them waiting for the right time, all the while my blood pressure was skyrocketing. By the time I was ready to let it go or talk about it, I would be mad enough to spit nails and use a few choice words that my mom would not be proud of. Anger can make us visit our dark side, go from zero to one hundred in a matter of seconds, say some things we will eventually regret and hold grudges until it's too late to say I'm sorry.

Despite the "I never get angry" badge we would like to wear, anger is inevitable. Recently, even though I thought I could and would handle the situation with tact and Christian love; it didn't happen that way. Before making the decision to talk about the issue, I thought I'd done all things right to avoid escalation. I had cooperated, tried to create a harmonious environment and even stepped aside to allow others to take the lead role. Nothing seemed to work. Even in my prayer to God for direction, the matter seemed to get worse each time I encountered the situation. When it was time to address it, I was hurt. I felt disrespected and frustrated; the seeds were planted; the roots were roots of anger.

Needless to say, there was no resolve. I had allowed anger to creep in and take over. Initially, my scapegoat was that even Jesus got angry. God told us we could get angry but there were conditions. I had met those conditions. As most do, I had only plucked up one scripture that conveniently made me feel better about my anger and that was Ephesians 4:26.

Because I thought I had done all the right I could do and wanted to speak my truths, I forgot about James 1:19; my dear brothers and sisters, take note of this: everyone should be quick to listen, slow to speak and slow to become angry. I had the wisdom to know I had been given the authority by the appropriate person so why didn't I adhere to Proverbs 19:11; a person's wisdom yields patience, it is to one's glory to overlook an offense? God knows our hearts and we cannot conceal anything from him; he knows the issues of our hearts and those things that cause us to lose focus on him and his word related to anger. We are free will spirits, so ultimately we have the choice to allow anger to take over or to completely yield to God's instructions. In II Timothy 4:5, Paul tells a discouraged Timothy to endure afflictions and continue to do the work. Iyanla Vanzant in her "Fix My Life" life-coaching has penned a phrase "Do the work," which in essence tells families in crisis to put in the work needed to mend their families.

Today, I'm admonished to make a conscious effort to "do the work" when it comes to anger.

1. Remember the less than pleasurable things that make us angry are part of the plan. Securing God's plan and purpose for our life is not always easy and comfortable;

2. Stop the need to vent your truths. Allow God's truths to prevail;

3. Don't give room to let pain, frustrations, and other things build up in your heart or mind; let it go;

4. Know that God created individuals and we must respect and love them in spite of our difference; and finally;

5. If we anger (we will; we are human) God can and will truly help us to reconcile the issue his way.

Inspirational Writings

Image

"I think it unwise for anyone to say there is an earthly, perfect image that everyone should mimic."

—Hope LeNoir

Inspirational Writings
Carmen Patton

I was 34 years old, and I weighed nearly 450 pounds. Now that's certainly an image for you. However, that wasn't the vision that jarred me out of my sleep. The vision that changed my life was the vision of seeing myself in a casket, my parents standing over me with tear stained faces. In the vision, they weren't aged, and I wasn't either. That image left me wide awake, breathing heavy with tears in my eyes. It was a dream, a nightmare, but it seemed incredibly real.

Daddy and I had gone to a Memphis Grizzlies game the night before the vision invaded my slumber. Since we're season ticket holders, every few days one could find me "squez'd" into that seat in section 112A at FedEx Forum. I say "squez" because it was beyond a squeeze. I was uncomfortable, and everyone around me was uncomfortable.

You would think this vision would have been enough to make me want to do better, but it wasn't. I'd grown quite accustomed to squeezing into office chairs, chairs at the beauty salon, and airplane seats and having those indentions in my skin from sitting in a chair that was too small (or rather I was too big for). I'd become immune to having to forego wearing seatbelts when riding with others because sometimes I couldn't get them to come around my 450-pound frame. Having swollen ankles and hands was now commonplace. So, the fact that the whopping one block walk from FedEx Forum to the parking garage left me sweating, winded, and needing a break wasn't abnormal either. Yet, I think it was that walk that particular night in the rain that led to the vision in my dream.

That night Daddy outwalked me. If I'm honest, at that weight, Daddy outwalked me every night. Of course, I place part of that on the fact that his legs are much longer than mine. However, my Mama could almost outwalk me too, and at the time, she had two bad knees. She is also shorter than me. Here they were, nearly twice my age, and they could outwalk me. That's a vision too. Yet, I still wasn't moved like I was moved by the image of me in the casket.

I had lost weight before. I had gone from 395 pounds down to 320 pounds a few years prior. However, I allowed the stresses of life, an unhealthy relationship with food, and a lazy nature to catapult me back above that weight and beyond. I'd convinced myself that I was happy in the skin I was in.

Sure, I was happy going into dressing rooms trying on the biggest size in the store and not being able to get it above my hips. I was happy being out of breath walking from the house to the car. I was happy sitting next to disgruntled patrons on airplanes whispering to flight attendants and suddenly being moved. I was happy being stared at in public places. I was happy being told that I was cute for a big girl. I was happy standing on the scale at the doctor's office and being asked if I knew how much I weighed because their scale only went up to 400 pounds. Yeah, I was happy. Shouldn't I be happy? I mean why wouldn't that make me happy? Isn't all that something to be happy about?

The cold hard truth is that I was miserable. Yet, sadly, I couldn't (well, maybe wouldn't is a better word choice here) admit it. Saying I was unhappy would be futile. I would need to actually do something to change the situation. I knew I needed to lose weight, but I had so much weight to lose. I couldn't walk a block, not a New York City or Chicago block; I couldn't walk a Memphis block without being winded. How was I ever going to lose weight? To top it off, even if I did, who's to say I wouldn't gain it back? I had lost 75 pounds and gained it all back, plus some. So, obviously, I'm a failure at losing weight. I'm destined to be fat and die fat. That's the mindset I had. That's the defeated spirit that I had. That's the dark place that I existed in until the vision disrupted my slumber that night in January 2012.

The vision pushed me back into the on again, off again relationship that I had with Weight Watchers. Food is my drug. I have an unhealthy relationship with food. So, in the same manner that so many recovering alcoholics attend Alcoholics Anonymous meetings, I attend Weight Watchers meetings. The vision helped me to see that my unhealthy relationship with food is eased with the weekly intervention of Weight Watchers meetings. I didn't want to die at 34 years old. I didn't want to be troubled with the high blood pressure and diabetes that plagued my family on both sides. I didn't want to be fat. I wanted to live. I didn't want my parents to live with the burden of having to bury their oldest daughter. I wanted to prove to myself that I wasn't going to be held hostage by my inability to control my weight. I wanted to learn how to eat to live, not live to eat.

Inspirational Writings

While I can't say that I've overcome the war with my weight, I'm no longer just sitting by idly letting it control me. Controlling my weight is an everyday struggle for me. I'm encouraged by those who are encouraged by my journey, but for me, it's personal. It's a personal war, but I'm fighting in the war one battle at a time.

7 Women 7 Words

Inspirational Writings
Hope LeNoir

Image is so foreign to me, or at least I want it to be. I want to look a certain way, feel a certain way, give off impressions a certain way, and I don't want to negatively judge another Image. So with this topic, I found myself in frenzied debacle. (I just wanted to use those two words together—*frenzied debacle*.)

My first thought of image was when my nephew and I sat in a car talking about whether or not God was a woman or man. My nephew believes God is a man. I challenged; God is a woman. I love to watch my nephew process and challenge back. I love to engage his thought processes. Even more so, I loved to engage his Image of God. Ultimately, what I believe is God is neither woman or man, but a Spirit whose gender (or non-gender) is what the body needs the spirit to be—whether that be father or mother, friend or guide, something visible but not human, or, as for me, a powerful existence that takes on many forms. That is my Image of God.

My second idea of Image came when someone asked me what motivates me to do what I do professionally. This was after a long corporate meeting. I replied, "Partially my niece. My niece motivates me to make this image visible. She has to have an idea of what this image looks like." As a little girl, growing into a beautiful woman, I want my niece to see an image of abundant, healthy success. I want her to know what is possible and how it is possible. I want to represent an image of an African American woman who is successful mentally, socially, spiritually, and economically. I want her to see an image of a woman leader of people and of persistent innovation. I want her to see a woman dancing in her purpose and happy working in her passion.

"But," I told everyone sitting around me, "I am just one image. I'm not saying I want her to mimic the image she sees of me. I'm not wishing she be something like me. I just want her to see this image while viewing other images. She'll have to make her own decision and craft her own image, but at least she sees what this image looks like."

And so I struggle with image here, though I love talking about Image in this realm. I think it unwise for anyone to say there is an earthly, perfect image to mimic for everyone. Maybe each image has a piece that when matched with a piece of another image and absorbed, can make one person spectacular. Even so, when it's all said and done, image is important personally and professionally. Let me tell you why.

Image, in the sense of "picture," "idea," or "visual representation" says a lot about you without you saying a word. Gone are the initial interpretations of, "I don't care what other people think." What other people think is absolutely important. Most successful people care how others perceive their image. This is also a confirmation of your level of emotional intelligence. This doesn't mean that one should always do a one-eighty based solely on what people think. It means he or she values what others think and can respond in the best way possible, out of safety, respect or simply consciousness.

Let me give a real life example here. Your image causes an interviewer to make an assumption about you during the interview. For example, an interviewer may wonder, "What does this person stand for?" "What is this person's personality like?" "Is this person conscious of the environment they are interviewing for?" One former executive once said to me, "The image the interviewee portrays lets me know if the interviewee even respects me as the interviewer."

All in all, image is important to you and for you. Be aware of the image of others and the image of yourself. Take a moment to reflect on your own personal image and note 1) if it is an accurate reflection of you and 2) if it is the best reflection of you. How do you do that? Ask around. Scroll through your Facebook timeline. Take a selfie. What do you see? Is it who you want to see? Is it sending the message you want it to send to others? Be big. Be bold. Take control of your image and the impact it will bring to you and others.

Inspirational Writings
Ciera Shannon

I remember a picture with twins. They had matching outfits and very colorful bows. They were smiling the same routine smile they had rehearsed time and time again for moments like this. Then there was me, unprepared with my play clothes on. My face strategically placed in the middle of my wild, bushy hair. My eyes filled with curiosity and loads of optimism. I was so happy to meet them. They were twins and their hair was decorated so beautifully, and mine, in what I thought to be boring, bushy ponytails.

For some reason they were intrigued by my wild bush. They insisted on rubbing their sticky lollipop fingers in my hair. I moved away a few times but the two were persistent, so I eventually stood still. One said, "Mama can you do my hair like this? I want it big and long like hers." The other began to unravel her twist and fluff out her hair in an attempt to replicate mine. She became so upset when she realized her hair wouldn't be as bushy, and for the life of me, I couldn't understand why. In that moment, I was proud of my untamed bushy mane. I felt pretty and unique. In that brief moment, I remember feeling beautiful and proud. I had something that other girls wanted. I was so used to it being the other way around. Fast forward a few years and several perms later…

"Chi Chi be still so I can finish. Don't you want pretty curls?"

"Yes, ma'am, but it burns. Can we just wash this part out?"

"Wait just a few more minutes' and we'll be done. Cortney, hand me that oil sheen so I can spray your sister's head."

Here it was, the six-week routine I had become accustomed to. The thing we did to look pretty. The thing I begged for so that I would be pretty like all the other girls. Ok, so it came with a few scalp sores. I was fly as ever and could rock shiny, decorated ponytails like every other girl in my class. This cycle went on for years, but then there was a transition. Mama had to work more, and I was eager to maintain my own crown. It started with braids at the front of my head and a short struggling ponytail at the back. It eventually morphed into me applying my own relaxer and when I say apply I mean by the end of the process my entire head was covered in perm. Yes, I know. Tragic. This ongoing application lead to split ends and toasted hair.

Fast forward to high school. This was my phase of fluffy curls and wraps. I had now perfected my hair toast by using marcels to style my hair immediately after application. I would use the marcels to make big curls all over my head at night and roll them with sponge rollers to finish. Come morning time my curls were popping, and my lip gloss too, but let's move on. I thought I was taking care of my hair but for some reason I could never get it to flow past my neck. The furthest it would go was to the top of my shoulders. I just figured my hair was never meant to grow any longer.

Fast forward a few more years. I was talking with a good friend, now my sister in law, and realized I had been applying my perm all wrong. I was only supposed to add it at the roots. I saw it on the box, every time, I just assumed they got it wrong. After finally following the directions, my hair grew an inch or so longer and that was it. So here I am, a sophomore in college, and thousands of hair toast later. My daughter is now four and I am hoping to get my life together. My hair is much healthier than it has ever been before. I am now applying relaxers every two to three months. My hair is much longer and desired by others. I thought I had made it as far as the hair department goes. What more could I possibly want? This lady I am now following, called the hair doctor, suggested we do away with perms and embrace our natural manes.

Ok, now, I'm all for hair growth, but I'm not trying to hear nothing about giving up the relaxer. You can have several seats over in the *Hell–to-Da-Naw* section, right next to the crazies. I'm with all she stands for, except for the cutting the perm part. My hair is thicker, shinier and all around gorgeous. I had finally made it. One day I'm walking through the student center, and I notice this girl. She's a beautifully mocha-tinted color. Her skin was glowing with a perfect shine, and her hair needs its own section for description. It was golden blonde with a hint of dirty but vibrant. It branched out from her scalp like a flower in early spring. She seemed unbothered and very confident. How was she able to do that? I thought this must be a hair piece, so I strategically found a table close to hers so that I could further examine her crown. So here I am stalking in the student center unapologetically lurking with my shades on. It's bright in there but it's not that bright. So I am finally able to get a closer look, and I can see it's not a hair piece. It's her actual crown. I'm sitting at the table like Kanye, "How?" (Inserts Kanye meme so we're all on the same page). First of all, how is her hair able to stand like that without any props? Secondly, how is she able to sit there with all this confidence and without an ounce of shame? Thirdly, who told her it was ok to deviate from the crowd?

I soon realized that these were all my own issues. I had lived a life in the safe zone. I was so stuck in my zone that I would even question those who dared to stray away from what I considered to be normal. I would often criticize others due to a closed mind. I felt that things should only be done in a way in which everyone was made to feel comfortable — even if that meant altering one's image so that other's wouldn't disagree.

Let's just say I have changed in that particular area. The girl from the student center is now my best friend. Embracing my crown was an obstacle I am so happy I faced. It not only opened me up to a variety of hair styles but a new found mental awareness. I learned to accept the person in front of me despite their choice of style. We have all allowed our preferences to cloud our judgement at some point. I am happy to say that this journey has allowed space for one less judgement.

7 Women 7 Words

Inspirational Writings
DiAnne Malone

2015 was an unsettling year for me. A conversation needed to be had with my sons. Especially my oldest son. The teenager.

I thought it only fitting my husband had it. He's better at these things. Teaching African American Studies for the past few years has not done me a good turn in these situations. He has more experience. Okay. You're right. He has more self-control.

Nevertheless, the directives must be given. The talk must be talked. We both, my husband and I, needed to sit down, and have a conversation with our sons about what to do should they be pulled over by the police.

This is not the vision I had for Neko, my eldest. When I think of his future, I envision a young intelligent man who is respected by… by everyone. I see an image of him, tall, the color of pecan pie, slim, and sprinkled with swagger. His image looms over me. It casts a cool, safe, comforting shadow, one I can sit underneath in my rocking chair and with my knitting. He will regale me with his college struggles and the way he met his wife, the perils of fatherhood. There would be no uncomfortable police/citizen fables of yore to be told. That would be over. Finished. America would not behave like that anymore. I thought that by now, these conversations would be a thing of the past. They are not. Now, because of the images I've tried not to see, because of the images I try to unsee, my vision has changed.

It's curious. I can actually see a better way of doing things, a better way of navigating diversity, like a luxury cruise liner, gliding across clear blue water. I see a better way of appreciating those manifold cultures and respecting the wonderful perspectives they bring. I can actually see Martin Luther King Jr.'s dream in my mind's eye.

After moving to Memphis, I gained a newfound respect for Dr. King. I must be honest; he had become a cliché. But Dr. King should be known as much for being a visionary, as he was for being a dreamer. I should be ashamed of myself for relegating him, no, watering him down to that two-by-two-inch image in my seventh grade American History book. He is more than an image. He was more than a dreamer. He had a vision for equality. He also had a well-thought out plan for achieving it. This is what many people do not know. His vision, his plan, helped achieve a dream. I respect that, because for a while, I was big on dreams, not so big on vision.

But vision can't stand alone either. Vision, for me, is actually placing yourself in a position to allow things to come to pass. But positioning is not enough. A plan is in order, because, really, what good is the vision without a plan? What can be achieved when you're walking around holding a baby vision in your arm, and not putting the vision on the ground so it can learn to walk. To run.

My vision, for my boys, is to be sure they do everything humanly possible to stay alive should their lives be held in the balance between one stray word from them and a purposed bullet from someone else. Notice I said humanly. I do know, God is in control. As a steward over my children, I am responsible for planning execution for the vision.

I've talked to them about this vision. I gave them a plan. I've gone over their rights as citizens. I teach them that respectability, knowledge of the law, and complete calm is necessary, but it doesn't guarantee that all things will go well. Neko's godmother, on the eve of his rites of passage and blessing ceremony, typed up the plan to stay alive, just in case he meets an ignorant cop. She laminated it. She placed it in a black box, and presented to him as if it were the recipe to a magic elixir, a potion for living.

Neko knows that all parents don't have to have this conversation with their children. Some young men don't need laminated elixirs that may or may not work. He knows because I told him. He cringed at it. He grunted and rolled his eyes; his thumb moved feverishly as he scrolled through his phone, looking teenager-ish and unconcerned. But I know it's a farce. He's seen the videos. He's heard the audio. He's witnessed the verdicts. He mumbled, "Mah, everything is not about race." He and his friend were pulled over by a policeman. It didn't go as well as it should, but it wasn't as bad as it could have been. The reason for the stop, the policeman thought my son's seatbelt was on incorrectly. He also thought the driver's 2004 Lexus sedan did not really belong to him. It couldn't belong to him.

Other details are not as important as the residue.

My son's face, as he communicated the story to me, is important.

The rite of passage has begun. I hear that it rarely ends.

His vision about the world, about himself, has changed. He is dogged and there is a familiar seethe lurking beneath those beautiful white teeth, on the fringes of his funny jokes, roiling around that boisterous laughter, playing tag with his laugh lines. His image changed after that routine stop. His vision has too. It has developed the voraciousness of a roaring lion.

7 Women 7 Words

Inspirational Writings
Demetria Adair

I have been in the business of personal shopping, fashion and image consulting for more than twenty years and one thing I know is true: every individual has different images they want to reflect depending on where they are; who they're with; and what the perception of the audience will be. You would think one's image would be stagnate but it's not. It moves, it transitions, it conforms. Think about it. There is the professional, friend-girl, parent, person without children, wife, husband, single person, ministry image, and the list go on and on and on!

We've heard clichés that imply seemingly perfect folks act different behind closed doors or vice versa. Yeah as I learned in Sociology 101 in my freshman year of college there is actually a social term for such behavior; it's called dramaturgy (look at the word and think about it). Without going through all the mumble-jumble of sociologist, basically we are all actors and our image conforms to the current stage. Does that sound like anyone you know? The study of sociology says there are three stages; front, back and outer. Look at image in those stages:

Front Stage Image:
This is the image where everyone is watching. Whether we are at work, at school, at church, in the mall, the beauty salon, at a sporting event, or wherever—this is the conforming image. We conform and adhere to what is expected of us by the audience or those who are watching in that moment and time. At work we are expected to dress, look, and work a certain way because our coworkers are watching—so we do. At school we are expected to sit, listen, engage when asked, and learn because our teachers are watching—so we do. At church we are expected to pray, praise, and recite because the pastor is watching as well as other congregant—so we do. At a sporting events we are expected to be excited about our team, cheer, and scream, because the coach, team and other fans are watching—so we do.

Back Stage Image:
This is the image when we are out of sight of the audience, and we are with other people like us. This is the non-conforming image. We are around our girlfriends, social club members, and family. This is the image where we can let our hair down, relax, laugh and not be concerned about what is or is not expected or acceptable; you can be yourself (whoever that is).

Outer Stage Image:
This is the image where you choose to be a part of an audience, you choose what type of audience and you choose the specific image you want to reflect to that audience.

Each stage of the world's image concerns the external person, and conforming to the world's acceptance. After looking beautiful, acting beautiful and doing everything you can to uphold the stellar outside image, what about the internal man? What about the image that God sees? Of course outer image is important; outer impressions can go far, especially professionally. So how can we illuminate an image that is both pleasing and acceptable to God and man? We can't. What we can do is follow the roadmap that has been given to us in His Word, which is specific in its instruction. "And be not conformed to this world but be ye transformed by the renewing of your mind, that ye may prove what is that good, and *acceptable*, and perfect will of God" (Romans 12:2). Also remember Psalms 139's declaration that we are "fearfully and wonderfully made" by Him and part of His perfect will for us is to maintain an image that reflects Him.

Hiedi Emily

In the 1990s a famous camera company had a very successful ad campaign with the slogan, "Image is everything." Part of their success was possible because we live in a society where outward image is emphasized. There are more magazines on fashion, hair, makeup, celebrity photos, and exercise than on any other subject.

This created a concerted effort in some churches to combat the image concept, declaring the slogan was a vain, ungodly message. I understand what they were trying to do, and I appreciate efforts to lift off of our youth the lie that their looks are more important than anything else. Let's face it, freeing all of us from the lies that your height, weight, skin or hair color, dress size, or thigh-gap (when on earth did that craziness start?) somehow define you. We're told we have to replicate some magazine cover that's been edited, enhanced, and touched up to be pretty. Why are we so eager to believe this image lie?

This image lie started pretty early in human history. "Who told you you were naked?" This was God's question to Adam after the fall. Adam had hidden himself and put clothes on because his image of himself had changed, and he was ashamed of it.

Have you ever considered this—he and Eve had the exact same bodies they did before they sinned. There had been no time to find a Ben and Jerry's and eat enough Chocolate Therapy to mess up their physique! For however long it was before they ate the forbidden fruit, they were frolicking in the garden freely, joyfully, and completely naked the whole time! They walked with God and were naked. Adam named the animals naked. Their sexual intimacy was pretty easy to freely enjoy, well, because they were always naked. All you present or former married ladies know when your man sees you in your birthday suit even when you feel bloated, or your hair isn't done, or you still have make-up smudges from the night before and sleep gunkies in one eye, it's on!

What is my point? The simple truth: image IS everything!

Going back a few chapters, the Bible declares, "So God created man in His own image, in the image and likeness of God He created him; male and female He created them." Gen. 1:27

Let's do one of my favorite logic exercises with this and a little additional information. It's called a Euclidean geometric proof. It's way easier than it sounds! Even if math was your least favorite subject in school you can handle it; I promise.

OK, God is perfect, right? This is a good place to have a praise shout and yell "yes" at the top of your lungs, unless you're in Starbucks reading this on your tablet. The screaming might be a little inappropriate in that case.
Back to our proof. God is smart, off the charts super smart, yes (that's wicked smaat in New Englandese)? He is also loving, patient, creative, relational, trustworthy, etc. Here's where the cool logic part gets great:

If God is all these wonderful things, and we are made in His image, then **we are all those wonderful things, too!!**

What a great image! No wonder the devil wants to steal the fact that image is everything and twist it to mean something it was never intended to.

Alright I hear some of you yelling at this logic proof I'm so very pleased with. You're thinking, "Hold on now. That was before sin, before the fall, at least two whole chapters before. We're not that anymore."

Are you a blood bought, born again Christian? If the answer is no, that can be remedied quite swiftly. Simply put your trust in Jesus by talking to him in prayer. State that you believe He came and died for your sin to pay your debt, and rose again. Apologize for that sin, and ask Him to come into your heart and life. The Bible says, "That if you confess with your mouth the Lord Jesus, and believe in your heart that God has raised Him from the dead, you will be saved" (Romans 10:9). It really is that simple. God is not nearly as complicated as some would have you believe!

If your answer is yes, then you are already a believer, so I have a question for you. *Who told you you were naked? How exactly does sin entering into the world negate our perfect God's ability to create you, or recreate you if necessary, in His image?*

The cross dealt with sin. Once again, God likes to keep it simple. If you feel like your image needs a supernatural makeover, Paul in the book of Romans explains that, as well. "For whom He foreknew, He also predestined to be conformed to the image of His Son, that He might be the firstborn among many brethren" (Rom 8:29).

This makes it clear that whether by creation or recreation (conforming) your image is a lock; it's sure and solid. Dear sister/brother, you are who He says you are! You haven't got an image problem, just a believing more of the truth one. And, yes, this too, is easy to solve.

7 Women 7 Words

Inspirational Writings
Rhonda Meydwell

Talking the talk of a Christian woman in the business world is fairly easy, but walking the walk is much more difficult. When I was first promoted into a management role, I was determined to turn that opportunity into a ministry. I spent a lot of time in prayer, thinking about what the image of a Christian woman in management looked like. Servant leadership as Jesus demonstrated to His disciples was my goal, but how does that work in a secular environment like the one in which I was employed? I had a small flock of ten young women of whom I had been placed in charge, and I hoped to do well by them.

During the very early days of my foray into management, I encountered a messy situation in which I witnessed true servant leadership in action. It was a sad story, really. I work in a large orthopedic clinic. We saw a lot of hurting and injured people, but we did not see many who were sick. A gentleman had come in to see one of our surgeons about alleviating some pain he had secondary to the cancer he was fighting. He was taking massive amounts of chemotherapy, and it was wreaking havoc on his lean body. Although he made a valiant effort to make it to the restroom, he had an accident in a prominent area of our lobby, and the evidence was there for everyone to see. With the help of his wife, this gentleman made it to their car, and they went home until he felt better to reschedule his appointment. Although filled with compassion for this man and his family, I was left with a very unsettling question of how the lobby was going to be cleaned. We had a cleaning service that worked after hours on nights and weekends—no in-house cleaning staff. The truth slowly dawned on me that there was no one in the building with the job description that entailed doing what it was becoming evident to me I was going to have to tackle.

Sure, I could have delegated the chore to one of my staff, but that did not seem at all right. Adding further distress, I was attempting to dress for success and was wearing a dress and open toed shoes... Finally, I decided that I just needed to get over myself and clean that mess. As I pulled on gloves and began to devise a plan for conquering this task, I heard steps behind me. Word of my predicament had made it around the building, and my CEO was standing behind me. Wearing a suit and what looked to be very expensive shoes of his own, my CEO began rolling up his sleeves. What was he doing? He was there to help. Together, my CEO and I tackled the unimaginable task in front of the lobby of onlookers. When it was all said and done, the excrement was gone, the floors were mopped, and I knew I had just witnessed true servant leadership in action. It was an image, and a moment, I will never forget.

Christian leadership in a secular work environment requires putting others' needs ahead of your own. It is never assuming that you have risen to a position too high to do the dirty jobs. It is demonstrating to those you lead, that you do so with a humble heart. It is demonstrating to a staff member who thought she had a nasty task ahead of her, that someone else is willing to take that burden. It is doing the job so well, no one can tell it ever needed to be done. It protects the dignity of others, and always recognizes the value of each person the leader encounters. For me it is also mentoring young women in entry level positions and helping them to grow professionally and personally. It is listening, it is (occasionally) advising, but most of all, it is truly caring about them (easy when you have a staff like mine). Christian leadership is service.

I rarely get opportunities to speak about my faith, my Jesus, or my salvation in Him in the workplace environment. My CEO is also a Christian, but I have never heard him speak a word about his faith either. We do not preach the Gospel in words at work, instead we preach through servitude. We humbly hope to lead by example, attempting to point to the One we ourselves follow. We serve those we lead by privately praying for our flock. We exercise patience, grace, and mercy to some who do not see these virtues anywhere else in their lives.

For me, being a Christian woman in the business world is all about image. It is about showing, not telling, those whom I serve with love, an image of the Christ I want so badly to emulate. At the Last Supper, hours before His death, Jesus did the unthinkable with His disciples, "when he had washed their feet and put on his outer garments and resumed his place, he said to them, 'Do you understand what I have done to you? You call me Teacher and Lord, and you are right, for so I am. If I then, your Lord and Teacher, have washed your feet, you also ought to wash one another's feet. For I have given you an example, that you also should do just as I have done to you'" (John 13:12-16). That—that is the image I want to represent me.

Inspirational Writings

Him

"As a woman I have learned I can never expect in him, what can only be found in Him."

-Rhonda Maydwell

Inspirational Writings
DiAnne Malone

"What do you want me to do?" I ask my son this, as he sits across from me in the passenger seat of the car. To turn and look in his eyes makes my back cramp. I rest my left hand on the steering wheel to keep my shoulder from slumping forward into an awkward position.

We are in the school parking lot. The day is a nice one. The car is small. The air is thick. This is where I learned my son was being bullied. At lunch he'd been called a horny little pencil dick.

"Mom, what does horny mean?" I press my lips together. Eleven years old and in the sixth grade, my son doesn't know what the word horny means. I am his parent, and I don't know how to tell him what it means, or even if I should.

What he knows is the word is bad. The boy who verbally abused my son has a bad mouth. A few days prior, he'd call my son and his best friend, faggots. I did not know the boy. I did not like him.

"I'm afraid if you come up to the school and say something, the teasing will escalate." Yes. Escalate. "I'll handle it myself."

"I support you," I said reluctantly, "but promise to let me know when it gets too much."

"I will." He said. I believed him.

I remember when I first met my son. Quincy. It took us a few days to name him. The Cesarean was brutal. Several blood transfusions later, I couldn't see him, but I'd heard him. Squeaking like a baby squirrel. Barely breathing. The size of my husband's hands. One pound. Nine ounces. Quincy was tiny but tough.

"How are you going to handle it?" I suck my teeth before I ask the question.

This is how I, his angry mother, would handle it.

I picture myself bursting into the school as the sixth graders file in for lunch. The security officer will trip behind me on her short legs and yell, "Ms.? Ms.?! You need to check in at the front office first!" I will throw my right hand in the air behind me, dismissing her, because I have come to save the day for my son. The cafeteria doors bang against the walls as I fly through them, just in time to see the boy spitting daggers from his mouth toward my son. My cape undulates behind me. I am Super-mom. I am on top of the boy, catching the daggers, using the daggers against him, mauling at him like a bear. In my fantasy, the other children he has also bullied are cheering.

"I'm going to ignore him. I know what he's saying about me isn't true. I can handle it."

Eleven and a half years ago, my son's primary care physician told me that I should be prepared to not see my son when I walked into the NICU. "He may not be there. He may be dead," he said. His body was under constant stress. He was not sure how long he could handle it, but he handled it. God handled it.

Every few days the boy would say horrible things to my son. "Shut the fuck up. Nobody cares about you." "Go kill yourself." "You're an idiot."

"What did you say, back?" I asked him.

"I didn't say anything. I just changed seats and ignore him. Some of my friends would say, 'leave him alone,' then, he'd pick on my friends."

"And then what would he do?"

"He'd follow me."

"Do you tell the teacher?"

"No."

"Why?"

"Because he's popular."

This is the stuff you see on the after-school movies, the stuff I never thought would happen to my kids. I'd watch the bullying documentaries. Even cry. *It won't happen*, I say. *Not to my children*, I say.

I have a tendency toward cockiness when it comes to them. Besides, I'd heard enough about bullying, the campaigns, the hashtags. I was bored with them, so bored I wouldn't even let the students in my composition classes write research papers about bullying. "It's a no-no topic," I'd say, pacing the floor of the dingy classrooms. "There is already enough stuff out there about bullying. I don't need to hear anymore."

Week two, my son bangs the trunk of the car closed after slinging his violin into it. He slams his body into the seat of the car, his lips taut, teeth locked down, the vein in his jaw jumping like a fish out of water and the water in his eyes standing at attention, threatening to spill.

"What happened?!" My oldest son was yelling. "Tell me what happened before we leave this campus!" He was getting louder and louder.

"I don't want to say it, now!" He yelled back. He'd already told my son twice; he didn't want to talk about it. Not now. "Wait until we get home, so I can talk to momma!"

"No! Tell us now. Tell momma!"

"Stop yelling at him!" I yelled at my oldest son.

"Look at him, momma! Something happened. That li'l dude said something else to him."

"What'd he say?" I was peering through the rear-view mirror at my son's clouded face."

"He told me to 'shut the fuck up, nigger…'"

"Nigger?!" I whispered, scream-whispered. No, that couldn't be right. Not now. Not in

2015. "Are you sure?"

He was sure. I was mad. The boy had gone too far for too long. I hated him for making me hate myself for not saying something sooner.

We sat posted outside the principal's office for ninety minutes, my husband and I. I tried to make jokes to keep him from seeing the water in my eyes. He turned his face away from me, to keep me from seeing his jaw pulsating. Were we bad parents? Had we scarred our son for life? Will he recover, be okay, after this?

"Why'd you wait so long?" The principal asked. Yes. Yes, we were bad parents.

"I was trying to protect my son. I didn't want the boy to retaliate…I mean, the situation to escalate." I dropped my voice, dropped my head. I was flustered—too emotional. My husband put his hand on my knee, which was bouncing up and down furiously. "I did what my son asked me to do. I was trying to support him—respect him, keep him safe. He promised he'd tell me if it got too much for him to handle. It got too much. Now, I'm here."

She nodded. She understood. I guess. I hope. She promised to take care of it. She did. But she couldn't, not fully. Some damage had already been done. I am in a constant state of repairing my son. Watching him close and letting him go, all at the same time.

"I've been through worse," he said with a crooked smile, his teeth crowding his mouth and forcing a grin, "remember, I was preemie. I almost died. I fought my way through that. I'll get through this." And he will. He did. We all did. We all do.

Inspirational Writings
Carmen Patton

He wasn't the same man that I'd given my heart and body to in 1996. He looked like him; well, he looked like a well-aged version of him. Seeing him still made me giddy like a school girl. He had the same intoxicating smell. His voice was still like a sweet country melody in my ear. His touch still gave me butterflies and made my heart skip a beat, possibly two. Eighteen years had passed since we first locked eyes at our beloved alma mater in Montgomery, Alabama. It had been about seven years since we'd seen each other. A random text in May of 2013 after nearly five years of not communicating was the starting point for this reunion. His support during the shock and grief of losing my godfather on my birthday weeks before helped to set the actual visit in motion. Now, here I was, over 350 miles away from home, in the city where we first loved each other. I was standing face to face with him in his driveway.

This image was different. Although so many things were the same, this image of him was different. He was grown. I was grown. He'd experienced things that were shaping the man he had become. Similarly, I was different. So, it was like getting to know each other for the very first time. He was my first love, and he was my first lover. He was also the first person to break my heart. Not this image though. That was the past. We were headed towards the future, and boy, did it feel good!

There were "Good Morning", "Just Thinking of You" and "Good Night" texts and phone calls. There were weekend trips and visits. I introduced my friends to this image of him so that they could see he was different. He wasn't the same one who'd made me cry countless times before because of lies and broken promises. I wanted to say to them you love me, so love that this image of him makes me happy.

I mean, who but God could be working this out? A person doesn't go from being dead to you to being someone you talk to each and every day. This has to be divine intervention. This has to be God's plan. God hasn't said he isn't the one. He hasn't told me this isn't His plan. He hasn't told me to leave him alone. He hasn't told me he isn't my husband. So, in my mind, in due season, God's going to fulfill His promise because that's what He does. Then, the shoe drops.

"My ex-wife called and we've been talking", he said. "I'm torn", he said. "I have feelings for both of you", he said. Wait. What?! My heart was breaking again. This time was different though. This time at least he told me. He didn't let me find out from girls whispering about me in the dorm. He didn't let me find out by seeing her in the car with him. He didn't let me find out by seeing her in his home. All of that was characteristic of the old him. Not this image though. This image was different. I knew the reconciliation with his ex-wife wouldn't work because God intended for *us* to be together. I would let him figure that out. It didn't work out, and I knew this was a prime example of a tailor-made blessing. He was mine. The image returned, and we started on our journey together again.

The image I had of us had me moving to Montgomery, being a supportive Friday Night Lights wife, having a baby (though he had two daughters already, a college student and a freshman in high school), and living happily ever after. As I sit here today, I can see that the image was all mine. Maybe he had an image, but in his I wasn't the character in the supportive Friday Night Lights wife role. I was that old trusty standby, loyal as a puppy. It's funny how the heart can make the mind fathom and the eyes see things different from reality.

I'd fallen in love with an image, a fantasy, a fairy tale. I'd committed my love, my unyielding support, my time, my goals, my prayers to an image, a dream, a fictitious reality. I could blame him, but it's really not his fault. He'd shown signs that he wasn't the image that I saw. He'd told me, without ever telling me, that the image that I had wasn't ever going to be. Mama always says, "You can show 'em better than you can tell 'em." He'd definitely shown me, time and time again. I'd convinced myself that God had brought us back together to be together. Yet here we are apart, and though I felt silly for playing the fool once again, I couldn't be happier about it. God is intentional in all things. He did have a purpose for letting me see that image of him. God used him to show me that I wasn't weak for having the image of him or any other man anymore.

Inspirational Writings
Rhonda Maydwell

The him I love is my forever him. There have been other hims along the way. All of the hims in my life have pointed me in the direction of Him—the big "H" Him. When I look back over my life thus far, I see a hymn in my hims. Directing me towards Him, there has been a rhythm, an order, and a sweet melody told in three parts—Father, Son and Holy Spirit.

This is *my* story; this is *my* song...

I am thankful for Him. Thankful for the Father. He knew me in my mother's womb. His plans for me were set before I was born. He wooed me when I did not yet know Him. His patience for me knows no bounds. He loves me the way I am.

I can see now, the many times that God beckoned me to know and love Him. There have been many hims along my way, on my journey to know God in all His glory. A teenage boy was one of the sweetest hims along the way. We worked together at a fast-food restaurant and attended different high schools. He was an enthusiastic Christian, and I knew nothing of his passion. He wished to share his love of God with me. Our dates were to Kansas City Youth for Christ meetings and Michael W. Smith concerts. This him was always kind to me, always respectful, always explaining the love of God to me. I tried to understand, but it was too much for me to comprehend. I was perplexed by a boyfriend who did not pursue physical affection. I let him pass... Him too, for a while, but I never forgot Him.

I am thankful for Him. Thankful for the Son. He is fully man, fully God. He lived a perfect life to show me the way to eternity. He demonstrates grace, so that I might extend it to others. He knew my sins would nail Him to the cross, and that, one day this would devastate me. His death and resurrection give me life.

The second him gave me reason to search for *more*. Young motherhood and a troubled marriage have a way of making a girl look around. Rather than love, this him spoke of a limited partnership and banned kisses on the mouth. I longed to be cherished. When it would not come from him, I sought and found it in Him. Jesus rescued me and showed me grace. He accepted me and set me on a path towards righteousness. The love of Jesus fed me in a bleak and lonely world. I do not blame or hold ill will for him. We both made choices. I am thankful for the him that launched my pursuit of Him.

I am thankful for Him. Thankful for the Holy Spirit. He is my comforter in times of despair. He gives me the gift of discernment. He intercedes for me when there are no words. He nudges me when I step off my path. He gives me power when I am weak. He is always with me.

The him I love today is my forever him. This him knew something about loneliness, but he also knew about a Friend closer than a brother. In friendship, this him always encouraged my pursuit of Him. This him never doubted that I would seek Him, find Him, and hear Him. This him encouraged me to draw closer to Him, taught me about Him, and ultimately proposed a three-way partnership: Him, him, and me. This him invites the Spirit into our home, our lives, and our marriage. This him entrusts our family to Him.

Yes, there were many hims along the way. Regardless of my spiritual geography during my journey, He continuously sought me and revealed Himself to me—sometimes through my hims. I continue to grow in Him. As a woman I have learned I can never expect in him, what can only be found in Him. My forever him is one of the biggest blessings in my life, yet my eternity is secured in Him—Father, Son, and Holy Spirit.

…praising *my* Savior all the day long.

Inspirational Writings
Demetria Adair

The initial news of her pregnancy is now a blur. I must admit, I was not supportive with my words. They all framed questions—How could you? Why did you? What will you? The litany was never ending. As the nine months of time progressed I seemed to regain some normalcy (on the surface), but behind the scene I went to bed EVERY night anxious, and woke up in panic worrying about my baby having a baby. My once "thick as thieves" relationship with my daughter was slowly becoming a constant negative banter between us—what I did younger than her, my disappointment in her, her resentment toward me for saying I was disappointed in her, me being sanctimonious, her calling me judgmental… The bantering was never ending. Oftentimes it seemed like time literally stood still. It was one of the most difficult, tempestuous times in my life.

I remember it like it happened yesterday, Sunday, February 22, 2015. It was cold, dreary, and grey snow clouds were looming. The prediction of snow and ice was imminent, and after being up literally two days watching my child in the agony and pain of labor, it was time. I tried to convince myself to be happy and remind myself that no matter what, this was indeed a miracle sent from God. All I could think about was, "She's having a baby. My baby is having a baby." Instead of focusing on the gift, my mind continued to focus on the hard work it takes to be a single mother; her dreams deferred, my dreams deferred, and most of all the lost innocence of my little girl after this experience.

As the five o'clock hour grew near, so did his arrival. The final push at approximately 2:15 p.m. brought *him* into my presence. For nine long months I had not acknowledged the reality of *him*, I would not get excited about *him*, and when I mentioned *him* it was only a facade of happiness. But this day, the icy stormy day on which he was born, all that changed. I had no choice but to acknowledged *him*, the reality of *him*; the beauty of *him* and the gift of *him*. By way of my daughter, God had given me a beautiful grandson who was whole, healthy, and perfect. He literally took my breath away when I laid eyes on him. This awesomeness is what I had resisted, because the journey was hard I had completely lost sight of how truly blessed I would be. Because of him I'm a better person and giddily proud to be his nana.

My journey with the acceptance of my grandson's arrival was a reminder that when God has something beautiful and purposeful for us, the news of it and the journey to get there is not always welcomed. What others think, say, or do as we make our way along the path can be a concern; the pain of the labor to bring forth the ordained purpose is not easy, but worth it. Birthing the end result of our journey's struggle is always a beautiful gift from *him.*

James: 1:17

Inspirational Writings
Hope L. White

Being a single woman, you eventually get to a point where you evaluate your singleness. This includes regularly going through the Hims on my potential dating list. It usually sounds something like this.

I actually didn't date Corporate Him, because I work with Him. I didn't find interest in corporate Him because the men I worked with didn't attract me. He was predictable and quite often, like me. Therefore, I didn't want to date me, predictable, the same, structured, confused. Nope. He wasn't for me, because he was predictable.

I didn't date Hustler Him either, though I was attracted to Him being emotionally far away. He was distant and I was enlightened. Perhaps being distant is comfortable to me because it is traditional to me. I was turned on by his emotional distance, though physically local, because that means he had issues. If he had issues, that makes Him distant, that means he is human. I know because I have issues. I am distant, and God knows, I am human. Though he was attractive because he was emotionally distant, I didn't date Him either, because he had too much mental and verbal distance that I was frustrated with. Mental and verbal distance brought about assumptions and uncertainties of what my status would be in the relationship. Nope. He wasn't for me then. He was too distant. Oh, he had a job. That was appealing to me, because that meant he had a goal, right? That means I can coach Him professionally and get a truck load of results for Him, but I can't date Hustler Him. So I just got paid to coach Hustler Him. So coach Hustler Him is what I did. I told Him to study hard and define his own image, place and destiny. I taught Hustler Him how to connect with the right executives and what type of conversations he should have.

Oh, as for the other Arrested Him, I told Him to look online for a job. I told Him to change his mindset. I told Arrested Him that just because he's got a felony and served time, it doesn't mean he can't get a job. Today. I told Arrested Him that just because he is a Black man, his ethnicity shouldn't be an excuse either. That was the hard core professional strategist that pushed people with potential to believe in themselves and just get it together.

Sure, I've read the *Invisible Man*. I've had a scholarly discussion about the *Invisible Knapsack*. Though I don't *want* to believe it, getting that job is harder for the third Him, the Arrested Him. I do believe it shouldn't have to be. Though not impossible, it feels impossible. And it is indeed hard. But, working harder to make the career dream work. Right?

Actually, I certainly believe in avoiding the mistake, which makes it easier to make the career goal. I believe not being in the wrong place at the wrong time makes getting the dream easy too. However, I believe it's impossible to always define the wrong place at the wrong time and it's impossible to assume before the wrong moment. What I also know for sure is making bad choices (not mistakes) makes getting that dream career feel impossible. I do believe there is a career game to play. I taught Arrested Him to keep playing until you win with integrity. Through all of that coaching, he still didn't follow through. Though not an excuse, Arrested Him is a tired, mentally abused, African-American, male and a felon.

Sigh. I digress.

Needless to say, through all that getting to know them, I never even considered dating Corporate Him, Hustler Him or Arrested Him.

Now Creative Him, he is an entrepreneur in life and in profession. I certainly considered dating Creative Him. Soon, I would be an entrepreneur, so the idea of dating Creative Him was on pause. I knew the literal time I put in my passion, the love I felt for my laptop, the concentration I put into every book, video and development tape. I knew the commitment I put into my clients and the joy I consumed when I saw their success. I know the high I get on the stage. Because my profession is my first love, I couldn't possibly have time for Creative Him. Not now. Right?

Then there's Well-Baked Him, who fell in love with the drive for my passion. He delights himself in my purpose and he runs the race when I see the distance. I am just like Well-Baked Him, I understand Him, appreciate Him, and know Him. So I love Creative Him.

Of course there is the Omnipresent Him, but my first Him too. Our relationship is above all. He knew me before I entered my mother's womb. He created me and designed me to be one of the magnificent ones. Omnipresent Him tailored me for a specific purpose to bring a beautiful array of nourishment and instruction to millions. Yes, Omnipresent is physically distant, but He hears my every word and sees my every mood. It is Omnipresent Him who is by my side in every situation, whether I want Him there or not. Omnipresent Him still loves me, even when I ignore Him. He consoles me. He gives me gifts, strength and health. For this and so much more, I love Omnipresent Him unlike any other. Through it all, he understands I still wait for another humanistic him. Ah, the complexities of all of them.

7 Women 7 Words

Inspirational Writings
Ciera Shannon

Broken, Battered, Misused and Abused. Left to be taken to the trash and disposed of. You came back. Despite these undying efforts, you emerged from the rubble with scars. Restored. Your pain is sometimes visible. Your smile sometimes forced. But giving up has never been an option, and I admire you for that. For years I have tried to hate you. Maybe a few years, I did. I did not want to understand you, and everything I did and said proved that. But there was a switch. A change that I could not deny.

I met you on October 16, 2013. I finally saw you, my Dad. It was strange. It was foreign. Painful but serene. In a moment of desperation, you finally fought for me like never before. For twenty-eight years I've known you, but on the twenty-fifth I saw a shift. You tried. It didn't matter if you were rejected. It didn't matter if I screamed. You sat there, and you took responsibility in the best way you knew how. That was enough. I wasn't ready for that. I was ready to fight and finally cut ties, but in that moment a light flashed.

That first meeting was casual but urgent. Sudden but genuine. I prayed for this day many times. I often would take that prayer back when things didn't go as fast as I wanted. I repeated this cycle for ten years. I would voice my forgiveness but immediately take it back whenever I saw a flaw. I wanted you to be perfect. You could never get angry. You could never voice concern, because in my eyes, that meant you were reverting back. I made up in my mind all the things a father should be. *He is kind, sweet genuine, and flawless. He does not have scars. He is not broken. He cannot feel pain. He cannot be hurt. He can never make a mistake.*

I was wrong. You are not perfect. You have scars. Your pain is sometimes worn on your sleeve. You have feelings. You can be hurt, and you have made mistakes. You will continue to make them. Acknowledging these things does not make you any less kind, sweet or genuine.

I remember going fishing at Martin Luther King, Jr. Park. The family talent shows. The foot scrubs and weekly arched eyebrows. The random dances to old school music and the lessons on understanding the lyrics. The boxing sessions and the unforgettable warnings about boys. You were the first to tell me that my husband would be my husband. You saw traits in him that I ignored at times. I am grateful.

There comes a time in life when you realize hardly anything goes as planned. In that moment you have to decide if you are going to wallow in expectations or accept and appreciate the authentic unfiltered version. For years I wanted to erase what was and replace it with what I thought it should be. Today I embrace the present and gravitate towards the restored being in front of me. Looking back is no longer an option. October 16th is now a holiday. I need you to know I see you. I love you, and you are appreciated.

Inspirational Writings
Hiedi Emily

Somehow seeing my soon to be ex-husband's Miracle Whip in the fridge after opening the foreclosure notice was the final straw. I hate Miracle Whip. The foreclosure notice on the home we had shared was still clenched in my hand as I hit the floor. This was the last thing to go. Since my husband had left and filed for divorce, we had already lost all other real estate property and the new conversion van that was the previous year's Christmas present (aka latest affair cover-up gift). The family house was the only material thing of any value left. "You did this to me!" I screamed it out at the top of my lungs from the kitchen floor while bursting into uncontrollable sobs. He did this.

I was trying to move on. Trying to hold it together in spite of the divorce papers served on my birthday. In spite of being maligned and attacked by the very people that should've been the hands and feet of Jesus at this time such as my pastor and some others of my church family.

You see our life had been all about him. I had just wanted to love and be loved. I wanted that happy family, nice house with the white picket fence, and a dog I'd heard existed when I was a little girl. But, I never got to experience that.

When dating he seemed so sweet and nice. He said and did all the things that made me think our life together would be that idyllic fairy tale. Now, as I faced having to find a place to live, and finding a job, I felt I would never know what having a good marriage and a happy home was like. He did this.

The truth is, I was only about thirty percent right. I felt like life was over and I would never be happy. LIE! I thought my husband was the him to blame. HALF LIE! I felt unlovable, ugly, stupid, and as cast aside as Tuesday's trash. LIE! I thought that there was no haven, no rest in this world for me which had caused me to briefly consider suicide. Big fat scary evil lie.

The truth was that the schemes of two very different hims were very much involved then and continue to be a part of my story. The him that really was to blame is the devil. The reality is my former husband was just a malleable pawn in the chess game Satan was playing out in my life.

The fabulous news is the third Him had been in my corner the whole time. Jesus heard every prayer and caught every tear I cried. He's the reason I survived the two times drowning had almost took my life. He's the one who drew me to Psalm 71:20-21 the day my husband left. He's the one that stopped me from killing myself the day my pastor blamed me for my former husband's infidelity, using Proverbs 31 as a weapon instead of healing balm. He's also the one who gave me the Holy Spirit the day I accepted Him. And the Holy Spirit gave me the strength that day to get up off the floor.

God guided me towards Psalm after Psalm on *praising* the Lord for His goodness, mercy, and love. Remembering that love and that Jesus really is enough, got me upright again.

In the years since, I have learned so much more about the greatest Him I've ever known. I've experienced his lovingkindness, restoration, healing, and leading. I've also learned a lot about why He chose to create me and the gifts, talents, and strengths he deposited within me. Perhaps most importantly, I've learned I'm deeply loved and I'm never alone. Jesus is always with me no matter what happens.

Because He's with me I'm stronger than I ever knew I could be! Because of Him I am whole and healed. Because of Him I believe and dream again—a modern version of my fairy tale. Because of Him, I am free. He did this.

Inspirational Writings

7 Women 7 Words

Help

"It wasn't that I didn't have help...That wasn't it...I hated needing help."

—Carmen Patton

Inspirational Writings
Demetria Adair

My grandmothers were helpers. They made things easier for us and others. They dealt with problems, aided and assisted, and they made things pleasant. Three of the most influential women in my life were always helping others. They were the anchors of our family, making sure everyone from their spouses, their children, their grandchildren, their great grandchildren, nieces, nephews, and even the neighbors' children were taken care of. They diligently worked in the church, community, and the schools we attended. These women were encouragers, defenders, teachers, and counselors. Annie, Willie Mae, and Frances were the picture of help in our world. Yet, there was another place where they were just as helpful and appreciated.

It began in the 1970s and lasted until well past the 1980s. It was a place and time where they rose early and took pride in what they were going to do; just like at home in our world. They were known as the maid, domestic worker, or help. I had the privilege to explore these places with each of my grannies, but mostly with my great-grandmother Annie (affectionately known as Momma Annie).

Before the now popular "take your daughter to work" trend, I went to work with my granny at least three times a week during the summer. Up before the break of day, she would make sure I was dressed and had breakfast (oatmeal or cream of wheat and toast). Similar to the ones worn by the ushers at church, she would then dress in the white pristine uniform which she had prepared the night before. We would leave very early, because timeliness was most important. We would make our way from our modest, clean neighborhood to what seemed like the land of the rich and famous (in some sense, it really was). Once we arrived and pulled into the long winding driveway we entered through the back door. My granny knew the secret place where the key would be for us to gain entry without having to ring the doorbell. As quiet as church mice, we entered.

The first thing on the agenda was to get me settled in the kitchen. "Don't touch." "Don't break." "Be quiet." Next she would grab her apron from a pantry closet and put it on running her hand across the front of it to assure there were no wrinkles. When she left the kitchen, and entered the bedroom of her lady (as she referred to her boss) I would watch her as far as I could see her. Once out of sight, I would listen closely as she greeted her lady in the bedroom. It wasn't just cursory conversation, she asked how the person was, how were the kids (she called them by name), even reminding them about appointments or just things to do in generally. My granny spoke with a tone of concern, conviction, and even authority (just like at home). For hours I would watch her dart in and out of the kitchen, busying about cleaning, washing clothes, cooking, and more. She was helping, it's what the Help did.

Some years ago researchers from Christian Brothers University in Memphis sought out my grandmother Annie (to this day I don't know how they found her). They were working on a study related to domestic workers of the 50s, 60s and 70s. They had at least two interview sessions with her. "Despite going to cook and clean, you were always so clean and polished; why?" "How did you feel about cleaning, cooking, and taking care of the families of others?" "What was your relationship like between you and the families you took care of?"

I remember her answer vividly and once resented it. Her answer was that although she was hired and paid to help, they, too, were her family and she took care of them as if they were her own family. Although she never knew my resentful thoughts, they were there. I thought to myself, "but they are not your family; they don't appreciate you like we do, and they certainly don't love you the way your *real* family does."

My grandmothers' humble beginnings as the help allowed them to plant many good seeds that harvested great returns. Until my Momma Annie's death, the children of the families she helped remained faithful to her financially, and more importantly, they kept *real* family ties with her. My granny received pictures of children, grandchildren and great-grandchildren of those families at least three times a year. She always put them in picture frames and displayed them right alongside ours. Not only did she have girl talks with us — but with them too! Not only was she our cheerleader, but theirs too. She attended weddings, graduations, bat mitzvahs, bar mitzvahs near, and far until she could no longer travel.

It was many years later before I realized the importance of my grandmothers' help for our family and her other families. Their work; their help had shaped many aspects of mine and my family's lives, as well as the lives of the Gold, Klein, Shulman and Creson families. Even today, I still receive the pictures of the grandchildren who are far away of the families where my granny was the help. The testimony of one of her children speaks passionately about my granny teaching her to play Bid Whist and checkers (the same games my children so fondly remember playing with my granny). My grandmothers made an art of the small things. The Bible says in Zechariah 4:10, "Who dares despise the day of small things.?" Zerubbabel had built the foundation of the temple which many thought was a small feat in the beginning. He also completed the temple, and the Lord was pleased with both the beginning and the end. My grandmothers began the work of building lifelong relationships by helping so many families other than their own; they completed the work by leaving a legacy of love, lessons and memories.

7 Women 7 Words

Inspirational Writings
Hope LeNoir

Ever toil so much your feet hurt, your back ached, your fingers were numb, your head ached, and your eyes were so red that maybe you couldn't see? You needed help, but you didn't know it until it was all over, and now you have nearly collapsed. Maybe it's just me, but I am betting that you have been there too. There have probably been signs along the way...

Maybe it was when a colleague told you to go home. Maybe you found your keys in the refrigerator. Yep. That was me. I'm changed now. I'm past doing too much.

Most of my life, my mindset was *just do it*. If it needed to be done, *get it done*. No one taught me that. No one told me to live that way. No one said that was the path to success. But without my mother and a father too far away, *just get it done* seemed like the logical thing to do.

Now I humbly ask for help. I realized lots of people would gladly help me when asked. When preparing for my seminars, speeches and other events, I reach out to get help, and in a matter of minutes, my resources are there. The weight is lifted, and I find more success than ever. Eventually people even proactively offer to help. I say *yes* more times than I said *no*. When I say *no*, I ensure I am making the right decision.

I encourage you also to have a *good* reason to decline when someone offers to help. Will you benefit from the help? Will the person offering their help benefit from helping? To this end, know that helping often brings joy to others. Some people find excitement in helping others. Others may find an opportunity to practice their skills.

Why wouldn't people want to help most of the time? Help is biblically translated as "to save" or "to be strong." Who wouldn't want to be a hero, savior, or strong person? Imagine if everyone was helping each other by using the skills given to them, whether at home, at work or in a spiritual setting. Imagine how smooth everything will go if everyone operates in their own strengths and passions. Requesting help is an opportunity to excel in a way that he couldn't have alone. Accepting help is a way to get ideas from others and execute more effectively and efficiently. Here is where you can envision a joyful space and realize an extraordinary outcome. These are all the expectations for professional or personal environment.

Don't wait too long to ask for help. Definitely don't wait until you can't hang in there anymore. This is something I have to remind myself of all the time. This often results in missed opportunities that you will regret later. Start asking for help early. This sets an expectation, promotes excitement and helps you feel calmer since you embraced a commitment early. Asking early also buys time in case you get a "no" or, "I can't." Ask people who you know enjoy doing what you need them to do. Ask people who are reliable and trustworthy. Be clear on what you need from them and why. Contemplate what's in it for them, and echo how your helper will benefit. Also be open to helping others too. Be proactive in offering your services, by letting someone who may be in need know who you are, what you represent, and how you can help.

Finally, express appreciation. If you're someone asking for help, don't treat people like a child or someone who is feeble and incapable. In addition, allow your helper to help in a way that says, "I feel privileged to be a part of what you are doing. I feel honored to be a part of your team. I'm excited about using my gift to help."

Help in ways that you enjoy. Express that joy. Use your skill. Don't help in ways you dread. This will make the experience less enjoyable and quite unsuccessful for everyone. Through it all, look forward to great success, healing and abundance through the help of others and celebrate the help that you can give to everyone else.

Inspirational Writings
Ciera Shannon

Even the strongest woman
Who can stand her ground in a room, full of naysayers needs help.
I am afraid most times but my mind refuses to allow me to succumb to my fears.
I could keep my mouth shut or say what is wanted
But the way my spirit is set up
 Everything is blunted.
Sharp, straight to the point, no nonsense, no chasers.
Some say this will be my downfall.
I have yet to learn to tame my tongue.
I couldn't sit silent when Sandra was murdered
Or when Darrius, Michael, Oscar, Eric, Jordan, Rikiya, Tamir ,oh, and Trayvon too.
My soul won't let me rest.
My body refuses to sleep.
The pain cuts deep, as if it is my own sibling.
You say all lives matter.
To be quite frank I find that statement redundant.
 The truth is in the press.
 Just because your dirt is broadcasted less,
 doesn't make it any less of a mess.
See if we're going to tell the truth, the absolute truth and nothing but the truth
Let's get to it.
Yes, you will be uncomfortable.
Yes, you may squirm.
But after this conversation,
 I pray that you learn this isn't about you.
I need you to comprehend that the gift of tinted skin
 does not validate the killing of an unarmed man, woman or child.
Maybe she shouldn't talk like that.
If only she had put out her cigarette he wouldn't have slammed her.
Had he only complied he wouldn't have been choked to death alive.

Maybe if his music wasn't so loud,
Or his pants so low.
Did you know he used to smoke?
Oh and he tripped a kid up by the jungle gym too,
about twelve years ago.
He has a criminal record.
He was bound to commit a crime soon.
You see this is what you do
Reverse the blame,
Shoot the bullets, and hide the gun,
Or the perpetrator.
God forbid it is ever your son.
Will you remember his birth?
That small tinkle of fear when he took too long to exit his mother's canal.
The moment he gasped for breath you vowed to protect him forever.
In a moment's notice,
Twelve years later.
 He is taken away.
Will you recall that time you yelled at him unnecessarily?
Would you boycott the selling of toy guns?
Would you demand the support of others?
Would you avenge his death?
Or would you look to the community for help?
Please express to me your reaction when you hear them
defile your baby with their agenda.
They did not understand him so they criminalized his very being.
They used his ignorance in youth as the sure factor.
Even if the opportunity of safe capture presents itself,
It would be ok to fire the gun.
Now remember this is your son.
They won't ask you about his character,
without noting his flaws before and after your explanation.
There is a great possibility that they may even blame you.

Inspirational Writings

So here's the question again.
What would you do?
When it feels as if all the odds are against you
Before the investigation even begins.
You're collecting your accolades searching for friends.
You're making note that your child once enjoyed reading.
Yes, and he liked fishing too.
He saved a dog once.
You now remember how he used to kiss you.
Before bed, school or that trip to auntie's house.
Now you're stuck on the couch.
Flipping through the news.
Praying that your child's deceased body isn't there to remind you.
That you are here alone and without help.
Your child is gone and they will soon move on to something else.
But not without first putting in a good word for his killer.
Now the pain cuts deep and you will forever remember.
What it feels like for the world to turn its back on you.
How it used your upbringing as an excuse to execute you.
Now here you are.
Empty!
Broken!
Enraged!
 Muzzled!
Where is the help when your entire world has crumbled?

7 Women 7 Words

Inspirational Writings
DiAnne Malone

It's a funny thing. I don't mind asking for help.

Okay, that's not really the funny thing. The funny thing is, even while I'm asking for help, I am working out in my mind how I can do it all on my own, so I don't have to take the help I'm asking for.

Asking for and actually utilizing help are not the same thing, and I'm working trying to change it. Here is why. I think the main reason we ask for help is because we have gotten to a place where we cannot do everything we set out to do. We can't do it alone.

The idea of help has been around forever. God acknowledged it right at the beginning. The garden of Eden was a big ole place for Adam to manage alone, so a helpmeet was made for him. Throughout the Bible, help was sent for God's people when they found themselves in a bind. There is absolutely nothing wrong with asking for help. Still, in my world of help, I ask for help amiss.

The biggest excuse used when you don't want to ask for help is, "I don't want to bother anyone." So what some will do is to try to do it all themselves. In doing so, it's easy to become stressed. Stress releases toxins that do all kinds of things like drain the body of energy, weaken the immune system, and raise blood pressure. Eventually, everything shuts down, and the things needing to be done have to be done by someone else anyway.

Asking for help, and not receiving the help yield the same results. From the very moment I ask for help, I boggle my brain trying to think of ways not to accept the help. I'm in panic mode twice over, and the very stress that should be alleviated is compounded.

Let's not forget when someone follows up on the help I asked for. "I thought you wanted me to help you with that? I was waiting for you to call me." My answer is usually the same, "Oh. I went on and took care of it myself."

In that scenario, several things have happened. First, I have people on ready for the help I asked them to give. Next, I drive myself crazy trying to do it without their help. Last, I communicate their help is not good enough for what I need. Those things are not what I mean to do.

I'm not the only person who does this. Right?

What I'm determined to do now is accept the help I've asked for, because, frankly, if I didn't need it, I shouldn't have asked. Most importantly, help fosters a sense of relationship and community between people, and my not accepting that is self-deprivation at its finest. I refuse to keep doing that to myself.

Inspirational Writings
Rhonda Maydwell

Whether you call it mentoring, helping, teaching, training, encouraging, or just being a good friend, God expects women to edify one another. And all of us encounter difficulties. It is not that I assume that those who have been in church since cradle-roll do not encounter difficulties, entertain doubts, or experience real suffering—that would be incredibly naïve. I do assume that during those challenging times in their lives, especially those times when they, perhaps, strayed from God's plan for their lives, that they recognize that tug from Him that leads them back home. Perhaps I am naïve after all. I am sure that what I assume, is not correct for many Christian men and women. The truth is, from time to time, all Christians need help remembering there is a God who loves them, has a plan for them, and offers salvation and healing.

Conversely, I have heard lifelong Christians lament that they do not have a really cool conversion story. To them, the testimonies of those who lived life on the edge, suffered through prison, or a dangerous life of drugs and crime coming to the saving knowledge of Christ is the ultimate. Extreme salvation! I am a woman who became a follower of Jesus as an adult and who does not have a super-cool conversion story (double-downer!), I am maturing into the understanding that regardless of how we came to accept Jesus, we all need help from others, along our path.

God gave me a heart for women and a calling to serve them early into my Christian journey. Early in my Christian walk, God showed me just how nurturing women can be to one another (when we choose to) and how much we can grow from interacting with one another. Several years ago, a new and floundering Christian, I found myself in Virginia Beach where I did not know a soul. The first thing God did for me in this strange environment was lead me to a believing friend, Elaine, who lived in my neighborhood. She invited me to a ladies' home Bible study, which was a totally new experience for me. These ladies put color-coded chapter tabs on my Bible and loved me further into the Kingdom of God. Next, God led my family to a Bible-teaching church that hosted a Sunday School class of women of all ages and diverse backgrounds. Let me tell you, I was *immersed* in the Word of God and nestled in the bosom of godly female companionship. I can honestly say I have never experienced sheltering such as that during my two year stay in Virginia.

It was during the in-home Bible study that I first learned of the concept of a Titus 2 Woman (TTW). If you do not know what that is, I highly encourage you to read chapter two of Titus in your Bible (it's a tiny book stuck way in the back of the New Testament). It says, in part, "older women must train the younger women" (2:4, ESV). The NRSV version of the Bible uses *encourage* instead of *train*. The implication is clear, however, that women are *commanded* to help one another. Since those Virginia days, I have always sought my own TTW. This is a mature woman who I trust to give me godly advice, to tell me the things I do not particularly want (but need) to hear, and to help me understand God's plan for my life. Some fifteen years later, I often find that I now serve as other women's TTW — a role I accept with great humility.

When I stop to consider the women God has placed in my path, I know that He intends for Christian women to help those who are less mature in the faith or are not yet believers. All of us need help from time to time, and all of us have help to offer. Those who choose to follow Christ look to grow in a continual pattern, and that is difficult to do alone (probably by design). It is my prayer for the reader that she asks for two things: 1) that God to lead you to a TTW who can help you grow in your faith, and 2) that God would lead you to a woman who could use a good mentor, encourager, and friend. Women growing together is more than a Hallmark moment, it is a Biblical command, and one that bears much fruit.

Inspirational Writings
Hiedi Emily

I lift my eyes to the hills — Where does my help come from? The Psalms echo the question of many of us. In a world that seems saturated with programs, self-help books, and a myriad of instructive options, could it be that getting the help we and our loved-ones need has been complicated by two main missteps? Firstly, we are often looking in the wrong place, and, secondly, in the issues and hectic pace of our own lives, we sometimes forget to be the help others need.

Let's take these one at a time. If we are looking in the wrong place, what's the right place? The basic first step to that is simple. Always look to our Heavenly Father first. Here are a few verses that show He is here for you and wants you to go to Him for help.

"I lift up my eyes to the hills. From where does my help come? My help comes from the Lord, who made heaven and earth. He will not let your foot be moved; he who keeps you will not slumber. Behold, he who keeps Israel will neither slumber nor sleep. The Lord is your keeper; the Lord is your shade on your right hand. The sun shall not strike you by day, nor the moon by night. The Lord will keep you from all evil; he will keep your life. The Lord will keep your going out and your coming in from this time forth and forevermore" (Psalm 121 ESV).

"So let us come boldly to the throne of our gracious God. There we will receive his mercy, and we will find grace to help us when we need it most" (Hebrews 4:16 NLT).

I recently was going over my financial plan and realized I needed to make some changes. I did a few things on my own and was getting very frustrated because nothing seemed to be making the difference I needed. Instead of trying to figure it out on my own again, I prayed about it. As I did, the Lord spoke to me about some future endeavors that will be very lucrative. While I was glad for the strategic ideas I couldn't see how that helps me *now*. With this on my mind, the Holy Spirit led me to a friend's house. I ended up being introduced to the immediate solution to my money issue because I obeyed God's voice! It came totally out of the blue, and is something I wouldn't have thought of on my own. Isn't God good?!

This leads into the second important thing to do when you need help. Look to be a blessing for someone else who needs help. The friend I went to visit that night had come through a cancer scare personally, and her children had both been very sick over the last year. We had prayed together for everyone's health, yet we hadn't had the opportunity to get together and just have some girl time. We had dinner, and talked, which is when what she does for a business came up. The Holy Spirit confirmed to me over the next three days that He was the one behind me learning that piece information, and this was going to help me in three different areas of my financial plan.

I wasn't looking to get help for me; I was looking to help her. When we choose to put our needs aside for the opportunity to help others, this gets God's attention. Aside from praising Him, giving is the most significant way you can enter the throne room of God on high alert for you in obtaining the help you need! Now, of course, I'm not suggesting to help someone just to get what you want; that would be a selfish motive. When you are genuinely reflecting the heart of God to put others first, and see past your own circumstances and pain, it makes Him stand up and take notice. After all, He "*loves a cheerful giver*" (II Cor. 9:7).

My help comes from the Lord, who made heaven and earth. The help you need is waiting for you. Be open to receiving while also being the hands and feet of Jesus to help others. It's Dad's circle of loving supply.

Inspirational Writings
Carmen Patton

The shame of it all made me sit on the step. I didn't make any noise to draw attention to myself. In fact, my friend didn't even know I'd fallen until she turned back and saw me sitting on the step with my feet crossed at the ankle, like it was a seat and I should be sitting there. Event staff rushed over and offered to call the paramedics for me. People in that section offered to help me up. My friend offered to take me to the hospital. I declined it all. I popped up like a jack in the box and tipped right on to my third row aisle seat. Anthony was going to come down that aisle singing "Sista Big Bones," and I was going to be right there dancing in it. There was no way in the world I was missing that. I sat through the concert and watched my foot swell as big as my head. I sat there with a flip flop on my left foot and my right foot on the floor because I couldn't get either shoe on it. The pain was excruciating. I convinced myself that I could walk to the car even though I couldn't stand to bear weight on it or put a shoe on it. I was wheeled out of the concert in a wheelchair, which was the first sign that I needed help.

Let's go back. It was a Saturday night, and summer hadn't quite begun but was well on its way. I wore a black maxi dress with a white shrug and a pair of black espadrille wedge sandals with a designer handbag big enough to carry a small child. Our seats were on the floor; they were third row aisle seats to be exact. We had to go down quite a few steep steps to make it to our seats. My friend was wearing stilettos and had a pair of flip flops in her purse that she changed in to before we headed down the steps. I had a pair as well; in fact, I had most everything I needed in life in that handbag that night. I didn't change in to mine though. I wouldn't need mine until after the concert when we headed out to get a bite to eat. She walked in front of me, and I teased her and said, "yeah, you betta take them shoes off; we ain't going to no hospital tonight!" Three maybe four steps later, I slipped and fell down two steps. Yes, I had third row seats, and I fell before the concert even began.

I didn't think I needed to go to the emergency room that night. My friend insisted that she would take me because my foot didn't look good, at all. I didn't want to be a burden to her, so I told her, I'd drive myself to the minor medical center the next day once the swelling went down. Did I mention that it was my right foot that was so swollen that I couldn't even stand or put a shoe on it? Yet I thought I was going to drive with it because I didn't want to be a bother.

She refused to take me home. So, I let her take me to the emergency room after a quick ride through Wendy's drive thru because we were hungry. We get to the hospital and had to hurry up and wait. The first thing we notice once we're in there is a sign that says you shouldn't eat or drink anything if you're there for treatment. So, I politely slid my food into that big designer handbag and snuck nuggets and fries out of it.

We stayed all night long. They did x-rays and told me that it was broken in a few places. I left the emergency room early the next morning on crutches. I was referred to see an orthopedic doctor for either a cast or one of those orthopedic boots (which is what I ended up with). Ironically, all I could think about the whole time with anxiety was: "Oh my God, I'm going to need help."

For six weeks I was dropped off and picked up everywhere I went. The first week I stayed with my parents because I was a complete klutz on the crutches. It wasn't that I didn't have help. Some people unfortunately don't have anyone to help them when they need help. That wasn't my case. I had more people than I could count volunteering to drive me around for those six weeks from family to friends to co-workers. I just hated needing them. I hated losing my independence. I hated having to ask people to take me places or do things for me. I hated being a burden. I hated needing help.

In my convoluted mind, asking for help is a sign of weakness, and I'm not weak. I don't want you to hear what I'm not saying. You're not weak if you ask for help, but I am. Don't try to understand it; just go with me here.

Then, there's the fact that I don't want to be a burden to anyone. See, in my mind, if someone helps me, I'm a burden to them. I don't want to be a bother to anyone. I don't want to inconvenience anyone. So, I'll try to do things on my own and figure things out on my own, so that I'm not a bother.

Asking for help humbles you. It puts you in a position to say that you're unable to do a particular thing without assistance. I'm very independent. In fact, in a lot of ways, I could be called Ms. Independent. I don't like to be dependent upon others. I don't like feeling like I'm beholden to others.

Inspirational Writings

Since I struggle with being humbled, it's obvious that I have an issue with pride. A part of my inability to ask for help has a great deal to do with my pride. I know, I know, pride comes before destruction. I, unfortunately, have self-destructed a time or two thousand as a result of my unwillingness to put the words *help* and me in the same sentence with *please*. I am a work in progress.

7 Women 7 Words

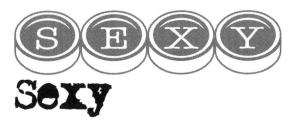

Sexy

"Sexy is an exercise in the senses...It is a reminiscence or a future hope... Sexy is as sexy does."

— Demetria Bowers-Adair

Inspirational Writings
Ciera Shannon

I walked past the mirror and something was different. I didn't care about the stretch marks on my breast, thighs or butt. My hair, coily and wet, half shaved with organic kinky roots up top. My skin, not the clearest, but my beauty is no doubt a statement. I don't know how to necessarily describe my eyes without sounding cliché, so I'll just say captivating.

There is a story behind them and, I know every detail. The good, the bad, the interesting and despite my knowledge of self, everything about me is sexy. The full lips I was once chastised about as a child, I now adore. They sit slightly off my face reflecting a combination of light pink and tan. My breast, full with milk requested from my son.

My stomach, my God my stomach, evidence of bearing life. She is traced with fair shaded lines and a darker widened seam up the middle. I remember crying because she had changed so much.

I am reluctant to gaze at my legs simply because they are marked with many scars from my past. The cut inside my left thigh raised and stretched from top to bottom from an encounter with a sharp iron gate. Not far up, a mark for smoking weed and getting caught. My spotted knees, darkened from life and an interaction between me and a red vehicle. I was ten. Oh, and the spider bite on the outside of my right leg that indents a little and has a slightly different texture. My feet were once a challenge, but now I can't seem to see what the problem was. However, they *are* in desperate need of a deep scrub and a loving pedicure.

I will not deny that I have my fair share of doubty days, but today, in this moment, I accept her. She is an undeniable beautifully flawed being. She realizes her unique beauty is something to be cherished and documented simply because there will be no other like her. Beauty is something measured in many ways. It is rare to see one celebrating without the permission of others. I now realize that there is and will only be one me. I will, without apology, celebrate and admire my physical self. I will do it in the morning, before bed, on my cycle, and when I feel just plain ol' ugly. I will write letters, take pictures, get full body scrubs and massages. I will drink water and an eat an abundance of fruits and vegetables.

What makes us sexy in this world of single accepted beauty and variety? Where will we find our place? Our place is right where it is. It is staring back at us in the mirror. It is flaunting your originality *without* the permission of others. It is smiling at your flaws and accepting their presence in this beautifully flawed world. It is unfiltered. It is steady. It is unwavering. It is you.

Being sexy isn't about looking or being like others. Sexy is being confident whether you are a size zero or a size forty. Sexy is knowing your worth and refusing to settle for less. Dare to be you even when it's scary. Especially when it's uncomfortable. But most importantly be you Every Day. Stay Sexy, Baby.

Inspirational Writings
Hope Lenoir

His face looked barer than I'm usually attracted to, and his belly was firmly round. His laugh was loud and awkward, and he was soooooooooo seeeeeexy! Her belly was wide, and every line in her back was visible. Her upper arms flopped about, but, my God, she was sexy. And me — I am a size sixteen, no makeup wearing, no booty, big thigh, permless, salt and peppered haired woman who is indeed — sexy. Believe it or not, all these sexy people are sexy because of their behavior, not their body.

Centuries ago sexy meant being physically well-endowed which indicated you did what it took to eat well. Decades ago sexy was being extremely slim indicating you did what it took to control your weight. Today sexy is being physically fit, again, indicating your display of control and security. In some places, despite the time, sexy is materialistically wealthy eluding to materialistic or physical security.

Research tells us that sexy are those things about our status and physical appearance that promise a future solid lineage and wealthy life experiences. For example, do our eyes line up just so? Do our hips suggest healthy childbearing? Does our proven ability to obtain money promise to take care of life needs? Does our attitude and behavior portray potential or success?

In my younger years Webster's definition of sexy was literal to me, and all church definitions of the word sexy was a true sin. In both cases the ideas surrounding sexy was wrong. Therefore, anything that was seen as sexy, was averse to me. It wasn't until I was an adult that I developed my new definition of sexy. As I grew older and more engaged in my career and business experiences, sexy became more than physical features. Sexy doesn't have to mean *sexually stimulating*. The Webster definition I find most fitting for Sexy, and have chosen to use especially in a business sense, is one who has interesting or appealing qualities.

You see, sexy comes with behaviors, choices, and attitudes — not just attire. Sexy brings the energy of smart knowledge, confidence, and doing the right thing for you. It is exciting to understand that sexy is speaking up sometimes but not speaking up at other times. Sexy is the decision maker who can make quick decisions with certainty, not because she is physically appealing in body, but because she is the decision maker with confidence. Sexy is playing your position no matter how quiet your position is. But, don't get it twisted, sexy is indeed visible.

As for me, sexy is not always speaking up, but observing, making the calculations, and simply saying one word at the end of decision table, *checkmate*. To me, Sexy is choosing not to eat three different deserts in one sitting, not because you're watching your weight, but because you are choosing to watch your heart and thyroid, knowing you have control. My sexy is also a smile. These are all the things that make me motivated and ready to move.

Sexy is a state of mind. For some people a sexy state of mind and behavior is often more challenging to commit to than a sexy physique. A sexy state of mind and behavior cannot be hidden. They follow you and are examined everywhere. Your physical being can be individualistic and covered in a group setting. Your behavior, on the other hand, is observed by many. No matter what you wear or where you are, your sexy is on display. Your job comes with your Sexy. How you interact with others comes with your Sexy. How you don't interact with others comes with your Sexy. How you express your dreams and aspiration plays a part of your Sexy. Sexy is determined by behaviors, choices and attitudes.

I've told you how sexy is defined. I've shared how I describe sexy, what sexy could be, and why. Whatever sexy means to you, wherever you are, go for the Sexy you're proud of and that defines you, and know there's nothing wrong about it.

Inspirational Writings
Demetria Bowers-Adair

Sexy is an exercise in the senses — it can be a thought, smell, vision, touch (or thought of a touch), or a taste. It is a reminiscence or a future hope. Sexy is a passing fragrance, a t-shirt in the laundry room, a fluffed pillow, a bathrobe, a simmering pot. A silhouette, running water, or a lit candle can heat up sexy. Being confident, self-aware, and powerful can explode sexy. Understanding sexy can take a lifetime.

As I reflect on my childhood and teenage years, I vividly remember the response from my grandmother if we dared to mention the word "sexy." Not sex but sexy. I mean my sister and I did watch Soul Train every Saturday night before bed, and there were some guys with smooth moves gyrating across the dance floor who wore their pants tight and shirts open way past the third button like the boys in school… So, yeah, the word sexy may have slipped out a few times. But where did we get the notion that moves, clothing, and daring to wear an open shirt were the epitome of sexy? Or for that matter, who told us that sexy had everything to do with the opposite sex? Who said so? Why then, and now, is sexy taboo?

Sexy is so diverse, such an enigma that I guess it could be taboo or generalized if you really don't know what it is. By the same merit, even if you think you do know, it's so different for everyone.

My matriculation (yeah because I started at entry level and graduated on a whole notha level) in the university of sexy has definitely been a journey and a learning experience. Entering as a giddy teenager with the perception of sexy based on the appearance of someone on television, advancing to a young adult where sexy became more than a perception but a personal reality attached to desires, needs, and love (yeah love) — the desire to be with someone, the need to have someone, and the love that I would share with someone. But, oh yeah, the next level; the one associated with entering the fabulous club of fifty — the empty nester club, and the best group of all the revelation club, sexy just becomes a beautiful array of many things.

However, we choose to view sexy, I don't think sexy can be placed in a nice neat box with an exact definition or limitations. Any negative stereotypes of sexy are the result of the term being so broad, yet so simple; explainable, yet unexplainable. Sexy is as sexy does.

7 Women 7 Words

Inspirational Writings
Hiedi Emily

There are certain images that come to most minds when you say the word sexy. For most ladies they would include things like soft lighting, candles, and lace, preferably with Barry White playing on the stereo. Others might remember how their spouse looked and acted on their honeymoon in some exotic locale. In general, beauty and sensuality is defined in the mind's eye of the person answering the question what does sexy mean to them.

How do you define sexy? If someone tells you you're sexy do you take as a compliment or an insult? Do you think you're sexy? Wow, I just had a Rod Stewart flashback (if you have no idea what I'm talking about, keep eating your Fruity Pebbles and go back to your cartoons, or ask your mother)!

To me being sexy is more than thinking you're pretty and desirable. It's an attitude. It's a mindset. It's a fact and it's a good thing. No, it's a God thing!

This definition might confuse some. Some might be tempted to think, "I thought you were a good, Christian woman. Single, too. Why would you say you are sexy?" I have run into this judgment in the past. For some the word has a negative connotation. Living in such a sex saturated society, a large segment of Christendom has gotten the idea that we shouldn't talk about such things. That somehow what the world at large thinks about sex being dirty and ungodly are true, thus, Christians admitting they're sexy is construed as wrong. It's so sad to see God's great gifts being relegated to the devil's distorted version of them.

Since God created sex, and specially crafted our bodies as men and women to be sexually complementary, and He said His creation is good, then being sexy is a great, God thing!

For those of us who are single, still awaiting that special someone, our sexiness is a little more reserved in order to preserve the fullness of this special gift for our future spouse. That doesn't mean, however, that we hide or squelch our sensuality. It actually is one of the ways that the right person will know you're the one. You're sensual energy, and passion will have a synchronicity to theirs.

I remember being in a season a few years after my divorce where I was very lonely, and longing for intimacy in every way. I asked the Lord to take my sexual desire away, and just allow it to be buried until the season for me to be married arrived. I guess I was asking for a hibernation of sorts. I asked pretty intently for a few weeks, but the answer I received was a clear "no." Even though that was at the least a few years before I would meet my future sweetheart (I'm still right here waiting for you, Baby) the Lord told me that my future husband needed me to be the way I was, and He wasn't going to remove any part of my sensuality.

In respect to married couples, you all are free to completely enjoy being sexy in all of its expressions. The great thing about couples who've been together for a while, is they don't need to verbalize the recognition of their spouse's sexiness and what it does to them. The perfect example of that is the look - you know the one. You could be at a party, church, or the grocery store thirty feet away talking about mundane issues with someone else, and that glance with a tiny sparkle in your eye let's your man or woman know it's time to leave!!

This highlights what I mentioned earlier about sexiness being partly your attitude and your confidence. In talking with those who have been together a long time I have also taken note that many men found the sweetness, confidence, and servant heart of their wives to be very attractive, very sexy, along with their appearance. In the same manner, many women I know while initially attracted to their husbands because of their strength, character, and confidence, say their husband's tenderness or selflessness in some situation caused them to know this was the man for them. And may I add that I and many of my single sisters find a man who'll pray out loud, worship with fervor, and excitely share the awesome thing the Lord showed him in his meditation time EXTREMELY sexy!

All of this demonstrates how being sexy is so much more than wearing lingerie to bed at night, or your special bra and panty set under your suit for that interview so you feel extra bombshell-esque (oh, yes, I've most definitely done that).

Sexy really is a great word that embodies the carriage of the woman or man of God who knows who she is, and loves and accepts herself as the great prince or princess of God she was created to be.

Inspirational Writings
DiAnne Malone

I got sexy in the ninth grade. I was fourteen.

A boy, way too old for me, but still a boy, saw me somewhere, doing some silly thing teenagers do and asked for my phone number. I had my own phone. It was cordless. A rectangular, white clunky something I'd talk on in the middle of the night, under hot stuffy covers, so my aunt couldn't hear me. I gave him the number. He called me all the time. He told me I was sexy.

I was so pleased with myself. I was pleased with my sexiness. The phone calls stopped as soon as the boy realized there was no sex attached to my sexy. It was cool. I had gotten what I wanted. A name for my dark skin, slim nose, braced teeth, thick hair, and tall lanky body. I was Sexy.

Some time after marriage, I forgot about being sexy. I had new names. Mom, Mrs., Moderator, Professor, Writer, Sister, Friend, Director, President, Student… These words crowded Sexy out. I got a glimpse of her and tried to retrieve her for this piece. I, like Justin Timberlake, wanted to bring Sexy back.

It was almost too late. These days, everything is sexy. Certain foods, like avocado, are sexy. Certain eating habits, like the Paleo diet, are sexy. Cars are sexy. I was hard pressed to find my way back into the world of sexy. I couldn't find *my* sexy. I did what I tell my students not to do. I looked it up online. It didn't help. Figures. Sexy's facelift made her unrecognizable to me.

Sexy is now equated with being on trend. Sexy is a fad. It doesn't make me feel like it did when I was fourteen and on the phone most of the night with that boy. So, at 44, I was mortified that I'd lost my sexy, and my efforts to get her back were almost fruitless.

I am not jaded. I know I'm not your mainstream beauty. That is, I realize that I'm not a "pretty girl" by measured media standards. My face is not symmetrical, it never was, even before I had Bell's Palsy. Still, somewhere in my growing up, a whole bunch of people convinced me that I would always be the most beautiful thing to alight any room. I wanted to get that feeling back. I wanted to seek it wherever it could be found.

On the eve of my 45th birthday, the Daniel Fast came to me in the form of sexy. I wasn't expecting that. I didn't really want it. Not that bad. Nevertheless, sexy re-started for me with Daniel and his ridiculous little fast (he and his boys were such show-offs!). No meat. No dairy. No sugar. No processed food. No yeast—which virtually means, no bread. Just pulse (food from the earth or from a seed) and water everywhere, all the time. No coffee. No coffee…

No. Coffee. I hated it, but I felt compelled to finish it.

My body rebelled against this sexy. If this was what sexy brought along with her, she could keep it. Three days in, my system shut down. Headaches. Crankiness. Tremors. Nausea. Insomnia. Forget this, Sexy. She required way too much attention. My self-control. Sacrifice. My ability to resist those tasty, delectable, morsels for which my body craved, thrived, survived.

Curse you, Daniel and friends, with your strong bodies and ruddy clear skin.

I argued that I was not an addict. Living only to consume those things that weren't good for me. Oh, but I was, addicted. Addicted, not sexy. I had to walk in that truth. I walked in that truth…for forty long days. By day 28, I knew what sexy meant to me.

There is not a skinny woman at the end of this essay. No before and after pics of scantily-clad-me poses. I'm a solid fourteen on a good day—a good sixteen to be safe. But I'm sexy. Day fifty. Still sexy. Today—still going. Still sexy. I'm friends with Daniel and his friends and the good Lord that made us all. We're sexy. I'm sexy. Even my food is sexy. The veggies look sexy on the plate. That green juice I just made this morning with a handful of grapes to give my lips a nice smack—that was sexy. I should be ashamed. I am not.

When I walk around, into, or out of my house, I feel sexy, because I've done the best thing for my body, and I can't stop doing it! I can't stop being sexy. I am not exaggerating. This sexy is the real sexy. I don't need anyone to affirm it, not even the boy who first told me I was sexy thirty - years ago.

Inspirational Writings

Woe to the person who comments, "You look great. I mean, you're glowing! What are you doing?" I share my journey. Some people balk; the corners of their mouths turn down. They don't want to hear about this forever new thing I'm on. I can tell some people don't even believe me. But, they engage my sexy stories, just to be nice. They raise their eyebrows in all the right places. They smile and nod. They say they don't have the will power. I say, "Yes! Yes, you do. You can do it! One day at a time." If only they knew how sexy being good to themselves can be. If only they knew.

7 Women 7 Words

Inspirational Writings
Carmen Patton

I'm sexiest when I'm doing things that make me happy. I feel sexiest when I'm walking in God's purpose for my life. I feel sexiest when I'm taking care of me. I feel sexiest when I'm eating right. I feel sexiest when I'm exercising. These are the things that give me a sense of accomplishment. These are the things that make me hold my head high. These are the things that bring me confidence. These are the things that make me feel sexy. But then I remember what does make me sexy. I may never have 36-24-36 as my measurements. I may never be able to wear heels and not look like a Clydesdale. Knowing that and accepting that is half of my battle in the fight to see myself as sexy.

Have you ever heard the phrase "beauty is in the eye of the beholder?" Well, for me, sexy is too. Sexy varies based on who you're asking. Sexy changes based on who's judging. Sexy can look different at different points of life. There's no specific image for sexy. Too many times I've seen sexy differ based on who's doing the looking.

The way sexy makes you feel is pretty much the same though. When you see someone sexy, you do a double-take. You feel a flutter in your stomach. Your heart pumps a little faster. You may feel a little nervous or anxious. Your mind starts to wander, and your imagination may ignite too. When you are sexy, you feel it. You know it. You live it. You walk it. You talk it. Your confidence is, as the young folks say, *on fleek*.

For the longest time, I had an illusion of what sexy was to me. He was tall. He was handsome. He was smart. He was funny. He dressed well—you know, GQ well. He was clean-cut and well kempt. He had an athletic build. His credit score was 700+. It's ironic. By those qualifications, I have yet to date a sexy man. Yes, I've dated men with some of those qualities, but all of them, no.

Then there was my illusion of a sexy woman. Her hair is always on point, not a strand out of place. Her skin is perfect, no blemishes. She's independent. She's smart. She's funny. She dresses well. Her measurements are 36-24-36. She wears four-inch heels and higher and doesn't look like a Clydesdale doing it. She's confident and secure. By those qualifications, I'm not sexy. So, you can see how the first time someone called me sexy, I found it laughable. The word sexy still kind of makes me uncomfortable now. Me? Sexy? Nah. Stop it.

As my life has changed, so have my views on what sexy looks like on a man and me. Here's when I realized that sexy can look different at different points of life. This is also when I began to embrace the notion that sexy is in the eye of the beholder. While some of the qualities remain, some have been changed slightly, added or subtracted altogether. I'm at a point in my life now where different things turn me on, and I don't necessarily just mean in a physical sense. Now, my physical senses have taken a backseat to my spiritual and emotional needs.

Sexy has now moved beyond what physically stimulates me. Physical stimulation doesn't feed souls. Physical stimulation doesn't nurture spirits. Physical stimulation doesn't pay bills. Physical stimulation doesn't calm fears. Physical stimulation doesn't encourage dreams. Physical stimulation doesn't take away doubts. Sexy now looks different to me. Sexy feels different to me. Sexy is different to me.

So, what is sexy to me now? A man who loves God is sexy. A man who understands the importance of fellowship and worshipping with God's people is sexy. A man who studies God's Word is sexy. A man who knows how to pray for me is sexy. A man who doesn't mind praying with me is sexy. A man who knows his role is to be my covering is sexy. A man who knows my role is to be his helpmate is sexy. That man can be short or tall. He can have an athletic build, be fat or skinny. I don't care anymore. Sexy has changed.

So many will read this and think she's a holy roller, and yet, that's the furthest thing from the truth. I simply know and can quantify what floats my boat now. I can say what sets my sail. What's sexy to me, may not be sexy to you. It's okay. Neither of us are right or wrong. That's the irony of sexy. See, it's like I said before, sexy is in the eye of the beholder.

Inspirational Writings
Rhonda Maydwell

Did you know that, despite how Hollywood may portray otherwise, that you cannot make a whipped cream bra and come across as sexy? No, it turns out, that when whipped cream squirts out of a can and onto a 98.6-degree body, it pretty much instantly turns into…milk. Sweet milk, for sure, and sticky… but it definitely does not hold its form so that you can walk out into the living room to surprise your husband with a whipped cream bra for him to, umm, remove from you… Is it just me, or is it getting a little hot in here? You see, I can report this to you with great confidence, because, well, because I tried it. This is just one of my many misadventures while attempting to spice up the ole "marital bed." There are others, oh, yes, there are others.

What is the first thing that comes to mind when I mention *biblical, monogamous marital sex*? Boring? Monotonous? A chore? Or HOT?!! If your answer was anything other than "hot," then you may not be doing it right! Sex is a pretty big deal, and powerful—the Bible says a lot about it, so sex is something we should take seriously. We barely get into the first book of the Bible, and in the second chapter, God spells out the meaning behind sex. "Therefore shall a man leave his father and his mother, and shall cleave unto his wife: and they shall be one flesh" (Gen 2:24). The word "cleave" comes from the Hebrew verb *dabaq* and translates, "to adhere, specially firmly, as if with glue." Sex is the glue that bonds two people. Have you ever accidentally super-glued your fingers together (I cannot be the only one who has ever done this)? It is very, very difficult to pry your glued fingers apart. If you force it, you are likely to lose some skin in the process. In other words, pulling apart something that has been glued together, *damages* what was once bonded. No wonder premarital and extramarital sex is a big Biblical no-no… Not because God doesn't want us to have fun, but because all of that bonding and ripping apart leaves us missing pieces of ourselves…damaged. God intends for us to be bonded to one person, our spouse, so that we can experience a special connection that teaches us something about how close God feels to us.

Sex is also a gift. It is pleasurable and feels good. If it didn't, then we wouldn't all be crazy about sex, right? And marriage isn't easy. We deserve a perk for doing the hard work. The book of Proverbs adds to the discussion, "Let your fountain be blessed, and rejoice in the wife of your youth, a lovely deer, a graceful doe. Let her breasts fill you at all times with delight; be intoxicated always in her love" (5:18-19). This passage doesn't exactly scream, "do your husbandly duty," or "check the box," does it? Husbands are encouraged to *enjoy* and *rejoice* in their wives. The Bible also encourages women to enjoy sex with their husbands. In *Song of Solomon*, the wife says of her husband, "Let my beloved come to his garden, and eat its choicest fruits" (SOS 4:16b). I am just going to leave that one right here for us to ponder…

Which leads me back to my whipped cream bra… I scoured the Bible for a passage that states that sex should always be performed in a particular position, or in the bedroom, or in a bed… Guess what? I couldn't find it—because it is not there. If you need some ideas from the Bible as to sexual scenarios between spouses, read through the Song of Solomon. You may want to have a cool drink and something to fan yourself with, because it gets pretty steamy in the garden… in the chamber… you get the idea. The idea is to check your glue and make certain that it is still holding well and to enjoy the gift of one another that God has given us. My whipped cream bra was a flop, and we laughed about it (laughter in the bedroom is very sexy, because it takes an immense amount of respect and trust to laugh during intimacy). My husband appreciates my Lucy Ricardo ways that begin with a heart to please him and to be pleased by him.

I would be remiss if I didn't address a couple key points that may have triggered sadness, regret, or shame in a reader. First, many of us have "damaged skin" from sexual encounters that fell short of the glory of God. Dear One, please know that our God is called the Great Healer for a reason. There is grace, forgiveness, healing, and restoration from past transgressions. God can create a pure heart in anyone the moment he or she asks Him for it. We cannot and do not have to allow our pasts to dictate our futures. We can enjoy, today, a pure relationship with our spouse or begin our wait for the one God will bring to us with a clean slate. Second, some men and women face physical limitations that make sex difficult or impossible. If this is the case in your marriage, ask God to lead you to find ways that you and your spouse can cleave to one another. Find that glue that cannot be broken. God has a design for your marriage, and it is meant to be a "specially" close bond and a gift.

The Cutting Room ~~Floor~~

The Words We Almost Left Behind

At first, there were ten. The authors would write up to 1000 words on each of the 10 words, and then, collectively, decide which seven words would make the cut. The caveat--all or nothing--all seven women had to agree on all seven words. What you've read in the pages prior are the fruit of that labor; however, the women couldn't let some of the words go.

There are more narratives, narratives fighting for space on the pages. Some of the cut material needed a pulpit. In light of that, a portion of the book is reserved to honor a few more writings that, while they were not chosen, are just as strong as the selected writings. The writings are from the remaining three words: **Vision, Retreat, and Still**. Hopefully, you will enjoy those offerings just as much (if not more than) as the chosen ones. From them spring just as much vulnerability, hope, pain and beauty. Enjoy.

Inspirational Writings

Still, Vision, Retreat

I ~~invited~~, no begged God to come back into my life, and HE met me there on the ~~wet moist~~ damp carpet.

                -Rhonda

VISION leads to destiny.

                -Hiedi

Retreat is discovering that ~~sometimes~~ sacrificing with quiet ~~is~~ may be worth peace.

                -DiAnne

Be still and know that I hear you.

                -Carmen

I consult the <u>Creator</u> throughout the day to make sure I am walking in the direction He ~~intends,~~ intended, for ~~my~~ the day.

                -Ciera

*Still is the time in our lives that God shows His ~~love~~—**UNDYING LOVE**—for us.*

                -Demetria

Don't walk or tip-toe, run with your vision!

                -Hope

Inspirational Writings

"Retreat" by DiAnne Malone

I was having a passionate discussion with my husband one night. I couldn't let something go, that is, I needed to keep talking until I felt as if I was completely understood. I needed a sign that my husband truly "got me," and until I received that sign, I would keep talking, not watching his eyes glaze over and him drifting away.

Later, I envisioned a beautiful dog who'd gotten hold to a small stuffed animal. That dog wrangled and wrangled the little teddy bear until the teddy bear fell apart. Overwrought. Under stuffed. Then, he –the dog--stood over it and lamented. He whined and whimpered, because he didn't have his favorite toy to play with anymore. He'd torn it to pieces.

I am the dog. I am often the dog. I don't know when to stop. Okay, I do know when to stop, when I tear everything to pieces, that's when.

My good friends know it. One hears me when I say, "I'm gonna let it go." She then says, "No, you're not." I say, "Yes, I am." She says, "No. You're not." Most times, I don't.

I am learning when to back off. Fall back. Retreat.

I'm not sure when this pattern of behavior started. Perhaps it stemmed from feelings of not being heard. Perhaps, I thought decisions I should have been making for myself were being made by someone else. Maybe I said to myself, "As soon as I gain some semblance of independency, I will be heard, and I will be heard fully!"

That is all just speculation. There are other viewpoints to explore. Especially for women.

We have taken a lot upon ourselves. We have had a lot to say, and no place to say it. We have become overwhelmed, and with all we have to say, we don't want to say that we are overwhelmed, tired, wearied, worried and worn out. We don't want to let up, because it is a show of weakness. We refuse to fall back, to retreat, for we feel with every retreat we are losing ground we've gained, a battle we've been fighting too hard for too long.

It is okay to retreat. Retreat is not surrender. It is a time for reassessment. It is a time to discern whether the battle is really worth it. It is discovering that sacrificing with quiet may be worth peace.

The last two years have been considered the year of the woman. We are on the come up. Hilary, Beyoncé, Oprah, and even Kim Kardashian have made it clear that women are worthy of several different crowns, and by hook or crook, we should ascertain and wear them. With the many crowns come a huge pain in the neck, because crowns, real crowns, with real jewels, are real heavy to carry. We must, rest on our laurels. We most disrobe and retreat in order to rejuvenate for when real battles have to be fought. We don't have to be on ready all the time.

I find there is pressure all around me to stay ready for battle. But, I am not made to operate on adrenaline all the time. I am not living in the wild. I am not running for my life from a big hungry lioness. I am a woman who has some level of control over how, where and why I should use my energies. I can decide on things, like when to retreat.

What do you have to lose, if you do?

Nothing. You've actually given yourself some extra time to regroup and get ready for what may be a more important battle. Besides, if you're weary fighting every battle, you won't be ready for the biggie (whatever that is). So, actually, a well-timed fall back works in your favor.

The word is, after all, re-treat. If you really want to get technical, retreat gives you permission to go back to where you had your best time, the best treat, and give that good thing back to yourself again! Don't waste time charging when you should actually be treating yourself again.

Inspirational Writings

The re-treat mindset has changed everything for me. Now, when having a passionate discussion with my husband I am dual processing. Do I need to have the last say, or do I need to re-treat? Am I really sacrificing a big chunk of myself in allowing him (or anyone else, for that matter) to have the last word?

If I tear up the teddy bear, I'll have nothing left to play with. Wrangling something to pieces is of no consequence. It only makes a big mess of innards for someone else to clean. And what's the real treat in a torn up plaything anyway?

7 Women 7 Words

Inspirational Writings

"Still" by Demetria Adair

Maya Angelou's *Still I Rise* is one of my favorite poems. As Ms. Angelou poetically lists obstacles, oppressions, and societal negative stereotypes, each line ends with, "still I rise."

The realness of life can and will make you question or doubt even the most definitive things in your life. Most of us have faced trials and obstacles that make us want to holla, throw up both hands, and give up, yet for most, giving up is not an option, and we find the strength to still keep pushing.

Loving a man since high school, marrying that man, and having life all planned out with that man, only to be faced with the brokenness of divorce after fifteen years was devastating and depressing. Frankly, the thought of reconciliation was beyond my view at the time. After sixteen years of post-divorce hurt, resentment, and blame, still God has reconciled us to care about each other enough to remain cordial and wish each other well, to be able to ask how are you, and to be able to laugh, love and celebrate our children and grandchildren.

Not having a job, the threat of losing everything, reading by candlelight for the unromantic reason that I couldn't pay the utility bill, trying to hold it together, and to not worry my family was a feeling of defeat. Still, God restored, and I am able to sit and look out my den window and watch the birds, sit on the patio, feel the warmth of the sun beaming on my face, or simply walk upstairs to my bedroom to enjoy a Lifetime movie.

To work faithfully in ministry, yet have my name, intentions, and work scrutinized is discouraging mentally and physically, and spiritually exhausting. Still God gives me joy, fulfillment, and favor when ministering to youth and serving the community.

Yes, we all face the challenges of life. Yes, we all have had our moments when we wonder if God is still with us. Still is the time in our lives that God shows his undying love for us. Despite what we are going through, He loves us and cares enough for us to restore, rejuvenate, and even eliminate—whatever our soul needs.

Through it all, still, God is in control. Still he gives us the strength to endure. Still he gives us new mercies. Still he gives us a way of escape. Still he continues to bless. Still he knows the plans for our life. Still he cares. Still he is good.

Psalms 107:1
Jeremiah 29:11

Inspirational Writings

"Still" by Rhonda Maydwell

Utterly broken, I sobbed face down into the fawn colored carpet of my small living room. The house was empty save for Moe, my rescue dog, a blue heeler mix, who laid quietly next to me on the floor. Even the dog seemed to sense that I was exactly where I needed to be, and he did not disturb me, but remained nearby. I cried out to God, "Still? Still, Lord? I abandoned You! I asked for some space. I am living in complete darkness, and You love me...still?" I continued to argue with God. I was no longer lovable. I did not deserve His grace, His restoration, or most of all, His love. Stubbornly, God kept speaking to my heart, "but, I do, Child."

It had been a rocky and lonely journey that had left me crumpled on my floor, physically drained from weeping, my red and swollen tear-stained face smeared with dried snot that had flowed as freely as my tears. To say that I had recently been through a miserable divorce is to only tell part of the story. The marriage had always been troubled. We had talked about divorce many times, but we did try to maintain the marriage for our children. I had become a Christian as an adult, after we had married. The more I learned of God's plan and desires for marriage, the more I felt compelled to keep trying. As time wore on, I fell into deeper and deeper despair. After several years of staying home with the children, when he told me I needed to find a way to support myself—I believed him. I got a job. When the conversation came that revealed neither of us had the energy to continue on with the marriage, I threw in the towel.

God was my biggest problem. I read Bible passages that talk about divorce over and over again. I knew I had what some call "Biblical grounds" for divorce, but that felt like getting off on a technicality. God hates divorce. How do contemplate something that God hates? How do I not? I remember that I was alone in my bed, Bible in my lap, and I bargained with my God. I said, "God, I am not sure if You are releasing me to go through with this divorce, but here is the deal. I need this. I cannot go on like this. I need some time to sort this out and to just do what I need to do here. If You will let me go to take care of this, I will be back." And just like that, He was gone.

I know now, He was never really gone. He was always right there, but I did not feel Him. I asked Him for permission to face the most devastating thing that had ever happened to me alone, and He acquiesced. No longer could I feel His presence or guidance in my life. I was lost and my life turned dark. I was anxious, sad, and angry all of the time. I couldn't seem to make a good choice for my life—and in my bleakness, I wondered if it mattered. Despair was to be my eternal future. The gravity of what I had done gradually dawned on me. I had divorced God. There could not be any coming back from a sin so grievous, of that I was certain. I could not even bring myself to go to church anymore—I was an imposter.

Many months passed, and eventually I was drawn back to church. I missed my Friend, so badly. I hadn't called Him "Friend" for very long, it seemed, before I had thrown away the best relationship I had ever had. I tentatively slipped into a tiny Baptist church filled with the most loving people I had ever encountered. My children and I were warmly welcomed, even if I divulged very little about myself or despicable condition. After attending a few months, and gaining some comfort, I signed up to participate in Beth Moore's Bible study, Breaking Free. I had done many Bible studies in the past, but this one is meant to get in your business—and it did. Through that study, and God's constant wooing, I learned that what I had done was to rebel. I had displayed extreme distrust in the only One who could never let me down. That Bible study was excruciating, but I was drawn to it every night until I ended up the soggy, spent mess on the floor. I invited, no, I begged God to come back into my life, and He met me there on my damp carpet. I felt His presence and, in my spirit, I heard Him whisper, "I never left you, Child. And the answer to your question is not still, it is always."

Inspirational Writings

"Vision" by Hiedi Emily

A well respected pastor in Texas has openly talked about how his mom helped him achieve his dreams through her own vision of God's plan for her son's life. She saw him watching the news when he was little, and as she prayed for him, God showed her that he was destined to make a difference in this world in ministry. He also has a beautiful singing voice. She encouraged his studies and love for music. He sang in the church choir. He wanted to be on the football team, but she said no. She wouldn't let his brains get scrambled because, she knew he was going to need them! She also was very selective regarding who he could be friends with as she understood his reputation needed to be stellar so he could be an example for others to follow. I admire him and am grateful for his testimony. He has traveled the world influencing others to be excellent and encouraging them to trust the Lord and his ways. He didn't get married until he was thirty-seven, and he waited for his bride to walk the aisle towards him as a pure man. That's right, he was a virgin on his wedding night! What a great testimony for the youth of today to hear. His mom had a big part in his purity and pastoral success. Having that kind of testimony is part of the vision God gave him.

Vision leads to destiny. In Proverbs 29:18 Solomon put it this way, "Where there is no vision, the people perish." Since God created us it, makes sense that He would know what is critical to our survival and enjoyment. Think of it this way, we are created in the image of the Creator. By definition this means every person ever born has some innate creativity with themselves. If we live our lives without finding our passion and giving birth to it through executing a vision, we have not truly lived.

Now I know some of you reading this might be skeptical. I happen to be a very crafty person. I love to quilt, write, and do many other crafts. I have friends who are musical, and artistic, or they create amazing things. Others look at our creations and think they don't have a creative bone in their bodies, but that's untrue. Creative vision can be found in any area of life. People who create computer programs had to start with a vision of what they were looking to accomplish. So did business moguls, athletes, chefs, city planners, and a host of other people. Creativity is really nothing more than the Holy Spirit inspiring someone with vision. Then it's up to that individual to choose to partner with Him to bring that vision to life.

People who dream and pursue those fine-tuned visions are happier, more confident, and often very successful in life overall. They also weather the storms of life more positively since often times, before a vision becomes reality, there are a few disappointments and failures along the way. Failing over one thousand times to make the light bulb didn't stop Thomas Edison—visionaries persevere.

When Proverbs talks about training a child in the way they should go it's more than teaching your children to know and love God and to be good people. Each child was created with a purpose, and as you help them dream and observe how the Lord has gifted and wired them, it's a parent's job to point them towards activities and opportunities that will develop and hone those gifts so they are ready to achieve their personal vision when that time comes. Taking the time to help them dream and then nurture those dreams is equally significant.

As adults we often try to balance family, jobs, faith, and community. With everything on the average American plate, it often feels like time for improving and executing our own personal vision, as well as, helping our kids discover theirs, is non-existent. Take the time. For your joy and fulfillment, your children's, and ultimately God's glory, invest the time in vision discovery, vision building, casting, and execution. You'll never regret the investment!

Inspirational Writings

"Still" by Ciera Shannon

Have you ever just sat in the moment and watched the world around you? Today we are so occupied with looking busy and trying to keep up with life that we refuse to just sit still and appreciate our very being. Lately I have allowed myself to get swept up in the popularities of life and I have lost sight of what it's like to just be. I often times reminisce about a family trip to Gatlinburg in the summer of 2011.

We were in a cabin, two cabins to be exact. There wasn't any cell reception and we all had to simply enjoy one another's company. Of course we had our silent quarrels, but they weren't big enough to distract us from the main purpose of the trip. I remember waking in the morning before everyone and sitting on the porch. The mountain view was so serene. The sun was slowly rising behind the mountain, the air misty with dew, a slight fog like in the movies and the best chilled air that I have yet to experience in beautiful Memphis, TN. I remember the quiet hum that managed to make its way through the house and spill into the outdoors. I remember wanting to stay in this space forever. In only a few minutes I managed to mentally photograph the entire cabin and surrounding area.

Everything was so beautiful. The heavily wooded porch with huge rocking chairs. I appreciated the shades provided at the end to porch for those wanting to soak in the hot tub. The glass door that led to the massive opening of the living room, kitchen, and a view of the upstairs. There was a door to my left that led directly to the inside porch. I admired that space so much but failed to thoroughly enjoy it for some reason. There were at least five sleeping rooms and a huge pool room upstairs. The place was nothing short of amazing. We spent most of our days chatting, exploring or just chilling, and it was the best feeling ever. I loved not having to be anywhere at a specific time or having to speed through the day in order to finish some checklist.

I can't wait to have that intimate time again. Now, here I am back in the real world, checklist in hand, requests waiting, with a stiff body and minimal peace. I am awakened by my alarm clock at 6:30 am. The day abruptly waiting for me to insert myself. I get up. I use the restroom and I immediately head to the kitchen to start breakfast for the little people. That's a hustle and bustle within itself. Because I have yet to organize myself, I am scrambling to print off baby girl's school work with baby boy screaming because he wants individual attention. It's only 7:30 am and the day has already gotten away from me. Quickly, 9:30am is approaching, and school has yet to start. I get frustrated about that which, in my mind, further sets me back and slows down my thinking process. School finally starts at 9:45 am. I am upset because it started so late and now school will end much later than I planned for the day.

Frustrated and looking for some mental relaxation, I pick up my phone and log into Facebook. I enjoy scrolling through to see how everyone is doing. I eventually get caught up in a recent post or article reporting about an injustice or an acquittal of an injustice earlier in the year. I am now even more frustrated and the rest of my day just feels tainted. I have operated in this self-inflicting mental storm for years after our family trip to the beautiful Smoky Mountains, until recently. I would reflect on those quiet moments randomly whenever I allowed time for myself until they weren't enough anymore.

I wanted to experience that sense of peace daily or, at least, four days out of the week. So I prayed and asked God for guidance. I sat in my floor one early morning and intentionally reflected on my mood and energy throughout that trip to the Smoky Mountains. I remembered my demeanor when I felt things were slightly off and how I was able to store them away, because they weren't urgent. I slowly began to apply that to my daily life. If it wasn't urgent, I didn't allow it to distract me. I woke up most mornings around 7:00 am or 7:30 am. I fixed the little people breakfast, and I allowed time for us to talk and just wake up. My husband finally convinced me to print off baby girl's work the night before and that helped out tremendously. I didn't feel rushed or run by outside sources. Soon I began to incorporate some stretching and morning meditation.

I began to feel more and more at peace. I limited my logins on Facebook to almost none, and instead, I read books to myself or my children. Instead of letting outside sources control my day, I chose to focus on my inward being. I noticed that I'm actually a pretty cool chic to be around, so I made time daily for myself. My days are still pretty unpredictable, and my alone time can range from fifteen minutes to an hour. I consult our Creator throughout the day to make sure I am walking in the direction intended for the day. I still have times in which I allow the day to get away from me, but those days occur less often.

Inspirational Writings

So tell me, how are your days spent? Do you allow your frustrations to distract you from a perfectly productive day? Are you so caught up in what isn't, that you haven't noticed what is? In those moments I encourage you to be still. Listen to your surroundings. Take in the noise of the early morning birds, the midday quiet, or the night time hum. Consult your Creator even for the simplest things. Know that you can change your current situation. Be Still.

7 Women 7 Words

Inspirational Writings

"Still" by Carmen Patton

Be still. It's said often to restless children. You know the ones that act as if they have "ants in their pants," as the old folk used to say. They're constantly in motion. Being stationary isn't an option. They've got to move even if they're just walking in circles and not going anywhere. They just can't be still. I often find myself like those children though. I don't necessarily mean in the literal sense. Figuratively, I can't be still. At 38 years old, I'm still a restless child—a restless child of God.

Be still, and know that I am God: I will be exalted among the heathen, I will be exalted in the earth (Psalm 46:10).

Be still and know that I am God. My inability to be still sometimes makes me question my own faith. If I trust God to know what's best for me, why can't I be still? If I trust God to have a plan to prosper and not harm me, why can't I be still? If I trust God to never leave me nor forsake me, why can't I be still? If I trust that He's working all things toward my good, why can't I be still? If I trust God to give me the desires of my heart if I delight in Him, why can't I be still?

Why can't I be still? Simply put, it's just hard to be still. It's hard to be still when you think things aren't moving fast enough. It's hard to be still when others around you seem to be moving, especially if they're headed in the direction you want to go or doing the things you want to do. It's hard to be still when you can see the end, but it's seemingly taking forever to get there. It's hard to be still even when you don't know what the end is going to be.

Being still involves waiting. You've got to have a measure of patience to be still. Being still involves being content. You can't be still when you're in a state of discontentment or when you're envious. Being still involves self-control. Your emotions have to be in check in order for you to be still. Being still involves levelheadedness. You can't be irrational and be still.

For some reason, I feel like God needs my help in order to bless me. I mean the second chapter of James says faith without works is dead, right? Works involves moving. Moving is the opposite of still. Yet sometimes your faith will make you be still. It will require you to have patience. It will require you to wait. It will require you to be content. It will require you to have self-control. It will require you to be levelheaded. Simply put, it will require you to be still.

Being still is often for your protection. Be still before you fall down. Be still before you bump your head. Be still, you're going to make yourself dizzy. Be still, we're almost there. Be still, and wait your turn. Sit down, and be still. A parent can be heard saying any or all of those phrases to a restless child. Likewise, I can hear God saying them to me.

When I'm seeking vengeance because I feel mistreated or wronged, I can hear God say, be still. When jealousy takes root in my heart and mind, I can hear God say, be still. When the spirit of discontentment takes over, I can hear God say, be still. When I get angry and my vile tongue goes into overdrive, I can hear God say, be still. When I'm working hard to get to something that He has clearly said no or not now to, I can hear God say, be still. When I'm trying to figure out what He is already working out for my good, I can hear God say, be still. When I focus my mind on what was or what will be instead of what is, I can hear God say, be still. When I lose my sense of direction and can feel my faith wavering, I can hear God say, be still.
Be still and know that I hear you. Be still and know that I designed you. Be still and know that what I have for you, no one else can have. Be still and know that there are no timetables on my blessings for you. Be still and of sound mind and good cheer. Be still.

Inspirational Writings

"Vision" by Hope LeNoir

When I walked past the door, I was reminded that I am a wealthy, happy, and all around healthy resource for personal and professional development who successfully equips others to produce desired professional results.

You see, on days I feel like I'm unproductive I read my Vision. On days I feel I am as quiet as a mouse, I am reminded of my Vision. How? Because I wrote the Vision down. I made it plain, and I hung it by my door. My written Vision reminds me who I am when I leave and congratulates me when I come back home. I wrote the Vision and framed it in a platinum frame (actually I pretend my frame is platinum). Every day, I am reminded who I am and the details of my Vision. Habakkuk 2:2 reads, "Write the vision and make it plain upon tables, that he may run who reads it." Because I wrote down my vision, it has become a habitual part of my life. Because it sounds nice, I actually run to make sure I manifest the Vision. I like that the scripture includes "run." Don't walk or tip-toe, run with it!

Writing your own vision of yourself is a great way for you to also claim and run in the success that is rightfully yours. Allow me to break down my Vision in an effort to help you shape and write yours. I said I am wealthy. I feel no shame or guilt in making "wealthy" my first description. Wealth, you see is having abundance.

Abundance is not just a lot of money and material things. Abundance will also manifest in a lot of growth, whether spiritual or psychological. For me, abundance is also the amount of opportunities available to speak to and influence many people or large groups. Having abundance is having the means to provide for family and friends in need, whether that is in mental or materialistic levels of abundance. Wealth also means having more than enough. I, like many others, enjoy having more than enough. More than enough to maintain myself in a way to help and be a testimony/example/inspiration to a million others. In other words, my intent is to be wealthy in an effort to provide intrinsic value to the mental and spiritual growth of people worldwide. However, in order to be wealthy, I must make wealthy decisions. My Vision is driven by an intention. My intent comes with deliberate choices. I must consciously learn, meditate, pray, and engage in my profession.

I also said I am happy. Happy is to be pleased or glad. In an effort to be pleased or glad, I must embrace those things that bring me pleasure and enjoyment. Knowing that my intent is to be happy reminds me to do things that make me smile and disconnect from things that will make me upset or that are not for the benefit of my spiritual and mental wellbeing. Accepting that happiness is my priority. I'm empowered to say "no" or "not now" whether that is "no" to things that will make me feel guilty later, or a new piece of furniture that will make me feel claustrophobic now.

Last, but certainly not least, I am healthy. First and foremost, "I am healthy" is a claim to my God. My life has been filled with sickness and disease. My past was filled with ill relatives and friends, so I now claim health. That is, I am all around healthy in mind, body, and spirit so that I can live long, give more than plenty, and provide a mountain of useful professional and motivational gifts to those around me and those afar.

It is through my past actions, mistakes, successes, circumstances, dark moments, and sickness, I am a wealthy, happy, and all around healthy resource for personal and professional development who successfully equips others to produce desired professional results. More importantly, my Vision is so because God said it. I'm reminded because I wrote it down. I made it plain, and I've made it visible to me every day. What is even more exciting is the other half of this biblical passage reads, "For the vision is yet for an appointed time, but at the end it shall speak, and not lie: though it tarry, wait for it; because it will surely come, it will not tarry" (2:3).

My Vision motivates me. It pushes me. It realigns my actions. It gives me clarity. It helps me make better decisions. Have you written down your vision? Have you made it plain? Is it visible to you every day? Are your goals aligned with your vision? If you haven't written your Vision down, take time to write down your Vision for YOURSELF today. Writing it makes it real. Writing it makes it doable. Research has found that 42 percent more people achieve their vision when they write it down. It gives me a reason to celebrate. Your vision should give you reason to make better decisions and celebrate too. Be proud of who you said you are and how it, your vision, will positively impact so many others.

Inspirational Writings

About the Authors

"These women flood the room with light as soon as their feet hit the floor. Their synergy is amazing. They are unflinching in honesty and generous in transparency. Ladies, thank you so much for bringing manifold blessings into the building."

-What we hope people will say about us.

Demetria Bowers-Adair

Daughter, **granddaughter**, **mother**, **grandmother**, **sister**, **aunt**, **niece** and **cousin**; **Owner** of Dainty's Fabulous Accessories and Women's Apparel and Dainty's Professional Services (one stop event planning);
Top three nominee for the New Tri-State Defender's 2013 Memphis Best in Black Awards for Best Women's Boutique and 2015 nominee for Best Novelty Boutique;
Personal stylist; for fab-u-lous clients who happen to be professional women;
Leader and founder; of a group of beautiful women entrepreneurial who wear pearls (Girls in Pearls);
Lover; of people, nature, food, chocolate, pretty things, clothes and shoes;
Sounding board, **soapbox**, and **shoulder**; for friends;
Advocate; for children, seniors, and the poor;
Organizer; of people, things, ideas, events;
Avid music lover; of all things Stevie (Wonder) and Donny (Hathaway);
Repeat viewer; of the movie Hangover PART I;
Encourager; of strugglers, pessimist, optimist, and fatalist;
Speaker; to an audience of predestined prepared to hear (by God) listeners;
Retiree; of political correctness and madness;
Former mayoral representative; for various human services boards (Metropolitan Inter-Faith Association Emergency Services, Senior Services, Coalition for the Homeless, Memphis City Schools' Adopt-a-School, Salvation Army Angel Tree Project, Memphis Child Advocacy, Shelby County Community Services Agency, City of Memphis Human Services Grant);
Adult graduate; of Christian Brothers University;
Testament; to God's restoration and reconciliation from divorce; brokenness of an absent father; the loneliness of singleness; and
Receiver; of God's salvation, grace, mercy, forgiveness and unconditional love.

Hiedi Emily

Hiedi Emily is an avid believer in putting words to paper to tell a story that inspires and teaches others. For more than two decades, she has committed herself to authoring poetry, inspirational messages, and short stories. As a Christian with the gift of teaching, she uses these words to shift the crowd she speaks to in a way they can leave with next steps for building their life in Christ.

Hiedi was the first member of her family to accept Jesus as her Savior. When you meet her, ask Hiedi to tell you about the moment she truly found Jesus a week before her thirteenth birthday. As Hiedi's relationship with God continues to grow, she follows her heart's desire to see other women walk freely and confidently in their full identity. Hiedi explains, "this book has been an avenue for me to be transparent about my journey so other women can view my testimony," because she knows others have been through similar challenges.

Though Hiedi is the proud biological mother of two children, Vannessa, and Daniel, she is a spiritual mother to many more in her community and in her church. She is "Grammy" to one grandson, Lucien. Hiedi serves as an altar minister, intercessor, Identity Coach, and a leader on the Freedom Team in her church where she loves seeing God touch lives miraculously as she prays and encourages them.

Hiedi has been a homeschool educator, Sunday School and devotional teacher to all ages, and a corporate trainer for the US government. Presently she teaches varied professional development classes at her workplace and through her company's charitable affiliations with local schools, colleges, and children's empowerment organizations. Professionally, Hiedi is a licensed broker for a Fortune 500 financial firm.

As an avid quilter, Hiedi loves to create prophetic picture quilts and American flag quilts for veterans. She also enjoys being active in and out of the gym. One of her biggest personal accomplishments is losing 120 pounds. She has been blessed to be awarded the Good Citizen of the Year award by the Daughters of the American Revolution, several leadership awards, and first place for the Toastmasters Humorous Speech contest. Born and raised in New Hampshire, she now calls Texas home.

Hope LeNoir

Hope LeNoir is the founder and owner of Rise and Fly ® LLC, a corporation whose purpose is to rejuvenate organizations and empower professionals through transparent, professional development coaching that will grow organizations and catapult careers.

Hope has coached hundreds of professionals and has been a speaker for and audience of thousands. She has been recognized for her career advocacy. She is the author of **RUSH** a book about finding your purpose in an effort to obtain and grow your best professional performance, positively impact the lives of many and promote stellar business operations.

During her own career journey, Hope has been an assistant professor, corporate financial services manager, financial broker, Corporate Citizenship Professional, corporate and nonprofit interviewer, blog writer and researcher. Hope is a member of several national and local organizations that promote the advancement of community, education and career growth.

She received her bachelor's degree from Dillard University and her master's degree from the Pennsylvania State University. In addition, she is a Six Sigma Black Belt.

Hope speaks and writes with authentic transparency. She is a believer of being true to herself and others so her audiences come out in a much better place. She is an advocate for greater professional and business expansion the right way. It is her core belief that everyone's strength's and gifts should be used in a visible way so that we can be fulfilled in a better professional space.

When she uses her gifts, Hope states, as quoted both on her website www.riseandfly.net and in her book *Rush*, "My heart pounds when I see my clients get great results and develop beyond what they ever imagined. This is how I know my purpose is to help professionals and organizations rise and fly."

DiAnne L. Malone

In her dreams, DiAnne Malone is sitting in front of a captive audience, waxing philosophically about her latest collection of essays, the last novel she wrote, her writing process; or she is standing behind a mic in the dark room of some lesser known pub filled with intellectuals, artists, poets, and members of the literary underground; there she performs spoken word, the kind that draws tears from one's eyes.

In her dreams, DiAnne is still tall, statuesque, and the color of a pecan shell. Her afro still billows rebelliously about her slim face. She still likes to play in make-up. She still binges on Netflix shows (especially the BBC ones). She still cooks. She still loves her only sister in a way no one would ever understand or articulate. She is still married to a minister of the gospel—who, even in tough times, makes the left corner of her mouth lift in the sweetest side smile; and she is still flanked on three sides by a teenager, a preteen, and a kindergartner, her children, Neko, Quincy and Layla, who, in her dreams, sit quietly, patiently, dotingly as she cranks out another ground breaking work of literary esteem.

In reality, she is all of those things. She is a writer of creative nonfiction, a few pieces of which have been published in noteworthy literary magazines. Along with her colleague, Dr. Cicely Wilson, she has produced several self-published novellas in a series called, *The Church Chronicles of Iris and Locke*. Her 40-day devotional, *Light Up*, was published in October 2015 and was inspired by her blog, "Who's That Lady." She has, as Professor of English and African American Studies, groomed poets, apprenticed with the likes of Rebecca Skloot and Joyce Maynard, inspired many fiction writers and orators, and mentored several women toward a life of fierce purpose and grace.

DiAnne Malone maintains a blog that is about seven years old. In between time, she navigates carpool lines, violin and choir practices, gymnastics, women's and children's ministries, public speaking engagements, and book collaborations. She listens to Harry Potter soundtracks through her earbuds while she writes and her children argue about who lost the remote. She writes a monthly marriage column for the neophyte digital magazine, "HIMPower," attends board meetings and accepts committee appointments. Her reality whizzes past her dreams into something ripe for adventure and rich with unpredictability.

All of these realities lead her to a life hanging in a beautiful balance between dreamscapes that, no matter how vivid and vibrant and colorful, do not compare to the reality she experiences from day to day. Her dream to touch the lives of many by culling together the talents of a few is fodder for the book you are holding. Her dream is to inspire readers to a reality that is more exciting and, strangely, more titillating than fantasy. In her dreams, your dreams, like hers, become reality and take you to a place you could never imagine.

Rhonda Meydwell

I thought it would be really cool to compare myself with a woman from the Bible most like me. What better way to introduce myself to readers than presenting a word portrait of who I am and how I came to be here? As is the case in many areas of my life, nothing about me is "cool," and I found, that my story does not neatly compare to one particular heroine of the Bible. I find I am a bit of an amalgamation of several women—which is just a twenty-five cent word for "big ole mess!" I am the sinner Jesus saved from stoning—one who knows what it is to mess up, but also knows of salvation. I am Mary, sister of Martha and Lazarus—one who often cannot contain her thoughts, feelings, and actions. When the Spirit prompts her to move, she moves...perhaps sacrificing her finest perfume in the process. I am also Martha, prone to be a little too busy at times, a recovering perfectionist. On my good days, I show my Mary Magdalene side—one who has learned to care little about others' judgmental opinions of her. One who is secure in who she is in the eyes of her Redeemer. She is busy and she makes certain that tasks are done and done well—the apostle to the apostles! More than anything, she is a leader of women and is willing to boldly guide them into the presence of her Lord and Savior.

Translated, this makes me a messy nerd trying to become the woman God wants me to be. I am many things to many people. I am Brian's wife and Christian and Katie's mom—and (gulp) a grandmother to sweet Georgia Kate. I am a writer. I am a recent college graduate from the University of Missouri (yeah, thought it would be a great idea to start college at almost forty) while I work full-time in a management position at a large orthopedic clinic, and not to mention the other million things a woman does! Are you beginning to see the Martha connection? I have lived some life, I am a sinner, and I have survived a painful divorce. I feel things deeply, and I have a flair for the dramatic. I tell awful (awesome) jokes usually involving terrible (fantastic) puns—I love WORDS! Jane Austen is my favorite author, and I don't care who knows it! I have come to a delicious stage in my life where I understand that I am not everyone's cup of tea (ooh, tea!) and that is okay. I do not need to be liked by everyone, but that does not keep me from caring deeply about others.

God has given me a heart for women. I love Women's ministries and Bible studies. I intend to write academic level Bible studies for women at home who ache to dig DEEP into the Bible. I know there are other women like me who love to chew on the meat of God's Word. Mary Magdalene, upon encountering an empty tomb, ran to find the apostles. She did not stop to ponder that as a woman she might not be taken seriously. Her Jesus was alive and people needed to know that and what it meant for their lives. If I am half the woman she was in her mission to spread the Good News, then my prayer will have been answered a thousand-fold. I know that God has given me a story to tell and heart that wants nothing more than to lead women into closer relationship with the Redeemer.

Carmen Patton

A HEAP of God and Family; A Handful of Crunched Numbers;
Two Parts of Non Minced Words; Pink and Green Sprinkles

All ingredients should be mixed together to make one EXTRAORDINARY woman, Carmen Renee' Patton. She's a Servant of the Most High King, a Daughter, a Big Sister, a Friend, a Sorority Girl, an Accountant, a Blogger of Basketball, and a Messenger for God through transparently sharing her own experiences. She's multi-dimensional, multi-faceted, and just an all-around cool chick.

Carmen was born the eldest of two daughters in the beautiful bluff city of Memphis, Tennessee. She was raised to believe in putting God first. Right behind God is family. To this day, she still lives by that rearing. Somewhat shy as a child, church was a place that Carmen was allowed to blossom. Though speaking before large crowds will still occasionally make her slightly anxious, it was at New Salem Missionary Baptist Church in Memphis that Carmen got over her fear of public speaking. She is a faithful member of her church where she has served as an usher for many years, dating back to her childhood.

Carmen loves spending time with family and friends and serving her community. She loves traveling and shopping, and often enjoys shopping time with her mother. She tries to travel annually with her mother and her sister whether it's a weekend jaunt to Hot Springs, Arkansas or a weeklong cruise to four different Hawaiian Islands. She and her father share a love for basketball; so, you can often find them discussing it or watching it together. Carmen is a member of Alpha Kappa Alpha Sorority, Incorporated, and through that affiliation, she has been afforded the opportunity to influence the lives of many through service.

Numbers have always excited Carmen. When she decided to matriculate to Alabama State University, she knew she wanted to major in something that would give her a career working with numbers. In 1999 she graduated Cum Laude and continued her education by earning an MBA from Strayer University, graduating with honors in 2011. Carmen has spent the majority of her professional career working as an accountant in Memphis doing financial reporting.

Numbers excite Carmen, but writing feeds her soul. Carmen loves to write, and she loves to use writing to fulfill God's calling on her life to encourage others, particularly women. In 2014, Carmen became a contributor to an all ladies blog dedicated to following and reporting on the Memphis Grizzlies basketball team. From there, her soul yearned to create her own blog, but she resisted that urge. She became a contributing writer to DiAnne Malone's blog, Who's That Lady during the summer of 2015. From there the urge to start her own blog grew exponentially, and shortly after her 38th birthday in August, she launched her own blog, God's Precious Pearl. GPP was created as an avenue for Carmen to pursue her calling of encouraging others. Her readers find her writing very transparent and relatable. GPP has also afforded Carmen to be a contributing writer for "A Message from God," a blog centered around messages from God with a God focus.

Ciera Shannon

Ciera Sicelia Shannon is Memphis born and raised, a true Memphian. She graduated from Hamilton High and continued her education at Victory University where she attained her BS in Psychology. There she carved out her place as a writer, poet, spoken word artist, fashionista, and standout in all forms of artistic expressions. Ciera's love of African American History sparked her interest in planning events in celebration of African American Heritage Month. She took that passion even further by becoming actively involved in her local community through the Memphis local chapter of "Black Lives Matter."

Soon after graduating college, Ciera discovered she had a knack for sewing. That discovery lead to the birth of her thriving business, "Cuddled Fabrics." She offers a variety of handmade items that range from infant clothing to men and women's apparel. Her specialties include uniquely patterned bowties, hair accessories, and African print themed maxi skirts. You can find her at various events in the community giving the people what they want whether it be merchandise, motivation, or love.

Ciera invests much of her time home-schooling her daughter Charia and son Chew. She offers them a varied education that incorporates African American History, society and culture, and health and wellness. As if that wasn't enough, Ciera finds time to encourage women of all ages and backgrounds. She has found a place on social media managing several pages that vary from topics on self- esteem, the importance of sisterhood, giving children a voice and making time for those you love. As an advocate for women who are victims of domestic violence, Ciera is a champion for women and encourages them to be self-confident, self-reliant, brave and strong. She holds these same truths for the young girls for which she advocates. Known for her no-nonsense and matter of fact tone, Ciera has developed a following who seeks out her frank voice and realistic approach to complex societal problems.

Made in the USA
Middletown, DE
09 October 2016